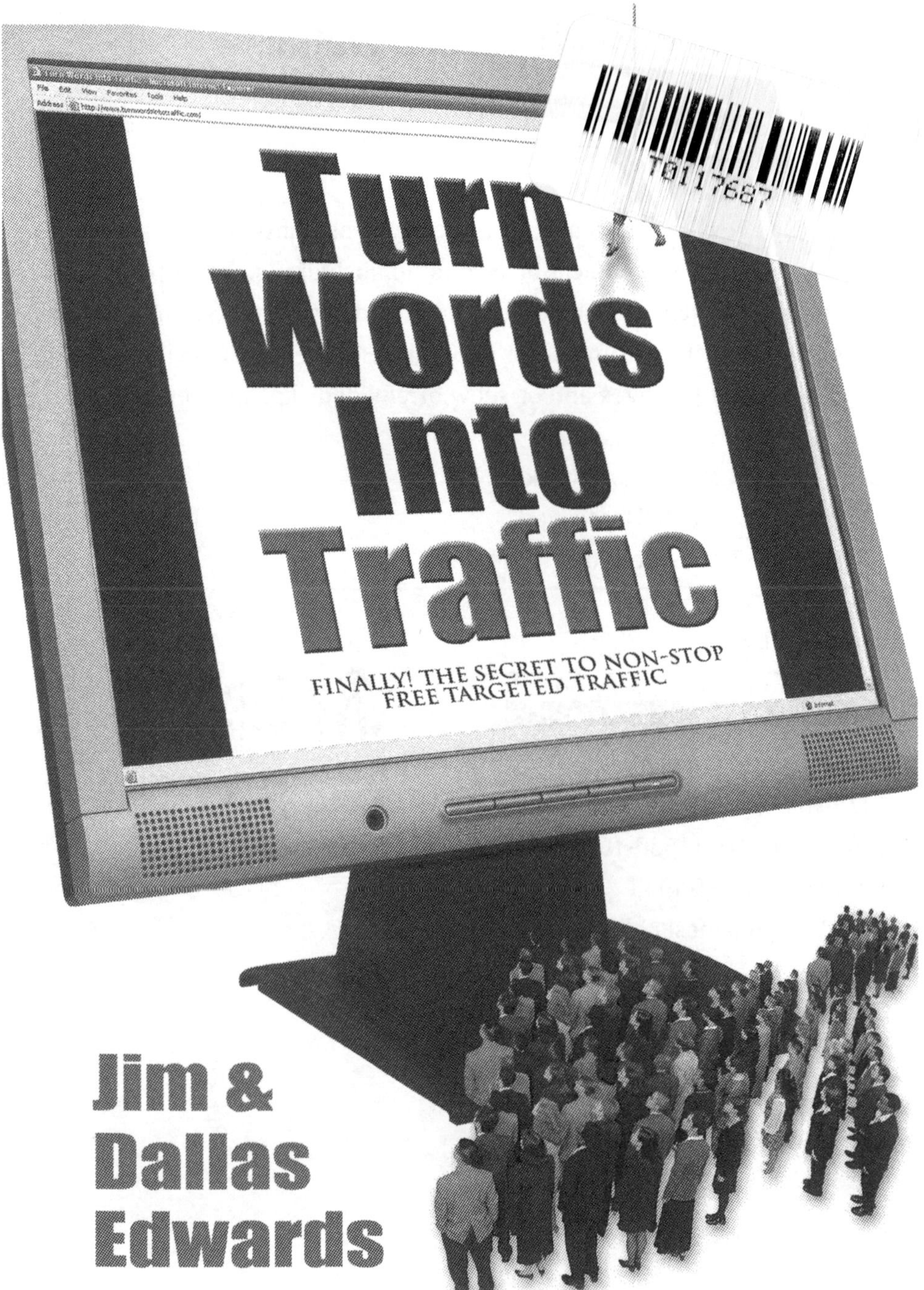

Turn Words Into Traffic

FINALLY! THE SECRET TO NON-STOP FREE TARGETED TRAFFIC

Jim & Dallas Edwards

NEW YORK

Turn Words Into Traffic

ISBN: 1-60037-151-5 (Paperback)
ISBN: 1-60037-187-6 (Hardcover)
ISBN: 1-60037-188-4 (eBook)

Published by:

MORGAN · JAMES
THE ENTREPRENEURIAL PUBLISHER™

Morgan James Publishing, LLC
1225 Franklin Ave Ste 325
Garden City, NY 11530-1693
Toll Free 800-485-4943
www.MorganJamesPublishing.com

Cover and Interior Design by:
Tony Laidig
www.thecoverexpert.com
tony@thecoverexpert.com

Limits of Liability / Disclaimer of Warranty:

The authors and publisher of this book and the accompanying materials have used their best efforts in preparing this program. The authors and publisher make no representation or warranties with respect to the accuracy, applicability, fitness, or completeness of the contents of this program. They disclaim any warranties (expressed or implied), merchantability, or fitness for any particular purpose. The authors and publisher shall in no event be held liable for any loss or other damages, including but not limited to special, incidental, consequential, or other damages. As always, the advice of a competent legal, tax, accounting or other professional should be sought. The authors and publisher do not warrant the performance, effectiveness or applicability of any sites listed in this book. All links are for information purposes only and are not warranted for content, accuracy or any other implied or explicit purpose.

Table of Contents

Author Biographies

Jim Edwards

Jim Edwards is a dynamic and entertaining speaker who has developed, marketed and operated outrageously profitable online businesses for both himself and his clients worldwide since 1997.

Jim writes TheNetReporter.com, a syndicated newspaper column helping "non-technical" people use the Internet for both fun and massive profits! Jim is a frequent guest speaker nationally at conferences and seminars on such subjects as search engine and directory traffic generation, "shoestring online marketing" and more.

He is the author and co-creator of numerous highly successful e-books, software and "info-products", including:

- **"33 Days to Online Profits"** and the NEW **"33 Days to Online Profits Video CD-Roms"** – learn to create a thriving online business in 33 Days!
- **"eBook Secrets Exposed"** – how to make MASSIVE amounts of money in record time with your own ebook.
- **"How to Write and Publish Your Own Outrageously Profitable eBook… in as little as 7 Days"** … even if you can't write, can't type and failed high school English class!
- **"Affiliate Link Cloaker"** – keeps Internet 'pick-pockets' from stealing your money.

- **"The Lazy Man's Guide To Online Business"** - How to Work Less... get Paid More... and have tons more Fun with your online business!
- Real Estate: **"Selling Your Home Alone"**, **"The TEN Dirty Little Secrets of Mortgage Financing"**

Jim lives in Williamsburg, Virginia with his wife, Terri, and five dogs. He enjoys writing, walking, playing video games, softball and listening to Frank Sinatra and Willie Nelson CD's.

Dallas Edwards

Dallas Edwards has spent a lifetime watching and analyzing how people do things – especially when it comes to written communication.

For the last 35 years Dallas has worked helping large and small companies get their acts together, stop wasting time and effort, and find creative solutions to their problems.

He spent the last 40 years perfecting his writing skills and has 4 offline books and 3 ebooks to his credit.

Over the years he has written hundreds of articles, papers, and essays for both his private clients and government contractors.

Dallas knows how to drive people to action and he knows how to teach you to follow his proven, fast writing methods quickly and easily.

Dallas' offline books include "**What Will Your Auto D.I.C.E. Roll**"; "**The 364 Day Year**", a novel; and the popular ebook, "**26 Key Typing Tutorial**", an interactive typing tutorial using subconscious mind programming techniques to teach typing skills in less than 2 weeks (**http://www.26keytyping-tutorial.com**)

Dallas also co-wrote "**The Lazy Man's Guide To Online Business**" with his son, Jim Edwards.

Among his other claims to fame, Dallas spent 2 years navigating alligator infested waters in Central America while serving in the Peace Corps.

Dallas currently resides in the Washington, D.C. area, where he enjoys reading, walking, teaching his granddaughter to play tennis and operating his consulting business.

A Personal Note To You From Jim & Dallas

As you go through this book you will see a short assignment at the end of many sections. You can either read the entire book first, then go back and do each assignment, or you can finish each assignment as you go and wind up with a finished article distributed all over the web at the end of your very first reading!

To help you, we included a section at the end of the article writing portion of the book that sums up all of the assignments. Consider it your personal "article blueprint" for future reference on all articles you write.

As with any great information, the action you take based on the information provides the real power to transform your life and your business. By actually writing and promoting with your own articles we don't just believe, we KNOW you can transform the quality of your business with a significant increase in targeted traffic to your website.

This book does not contain one ounce of theory. We've proven everything contained in this book through action, sweat, mistakes and ultimate triumphs. Everything you read has been rigorously tested and proven true through tens-of-thousands of website visitors, thousands of sales, and hundreds of articles.

"Don't teach what you don't know... don't lead where you don't go!" always seemed a wise motto to us.

Other than free search engines, publishing articles represents the last truly effective "FREE" way to get valuable, targeted traffic to your site. And, unlike free search engines, promoting with articles doesn't require any special skills, programming or "magic spells" to make it effective.

Learn these techniques for writing and promoting your business with articles, apply them, and in a relatively short time you'll see your traffic logs swell with targeted, ready-to-buy traffic!

To your success!

Jim & Dallas Edwards

"The Stonecutter"

Before we get into the actual article writing process, let's set the stage for you to understand the "big picture" when it comes to writing articles, promoting with them and using them to bring qualified, targeted traffic to your website.

We think this classic story explains it best.

Once upon a time…

A man not much different from you and us worked extremely hard as a stonecutter. This man lived long before the invention of explosives or modern machinery, so he cut stones the old fashioned way – by swinging a great big sledgehammer against the rocks until they broke.

People would hire the stonecutter to come to their property and break up large stones into small pieces so they could cart them away. When someone hired him he would arrive at their property and day after day he would beat on the huge boulders. Sometimes it took only a morning to break up the rock and other times it took weeks.

One day, while he methodically hammered away at a huge boulder, he struck what seemed like a mighty blow and the stone splintered into a hundred pieces. The young son of the landowner rushed up to the stonecutter and exclaimed, "WOW! You broke that huge boulder into a million pieces. You sure must be strong to have done that with one swing of your hammer!"

The stonecutter smiled, patted the boy on the head, and said, "I appreciate the compliment, but you need to understand something very

important. It wasn't that one blow that did it. It was all the blows together over the last few weeks that added up to what looked like a single mighty swing!

"All the effort that came before finally paid off on that last hit. But the truth is, I didn't know how many swings it would take to break the rock, so I had to take them all!"

At this point you may wonder, "What the heck does this stonecutter story have to do with writing articles and using them to promote my website?"

Well, actually it sums up the entire article writing and promotion process perfectly in just a few paragraphs.

When you promote with articles you never quite know which one will have virtually every ezine editor or website owner you approach, scrambling to publish it for their subscribers. You just keep on plugging, because as you go along each article builds upon the last.

By following the advice laid out in this book you will learn to use articles to create streams of traffic to your website. Some will create huge streams while others bring just a few visitors a day. But, collectively, all your articles added up will eventually "break the boulder" to drive your website traffic logs wild!

You don't know which article will do it. Your first could do it (it certainly does happen)... or your 20th article could do it. But you need to understand right now that **only good things come out of writing articles**.

The following represents the worst-case scenario from every article you ever write. (By the way, we wish every "downside" looked this good!)

By writing, publishing and promoting with articles:

- You continue to build your reputation with your target audience as a trusted expert.
- As your credibility increases, "Joint Venture" partners will begin to seek you out and open up to your approaches.

- You'll create additional tools your affiliates can use to sell more of your products. You can also use your articles to recruit NEW, high-quality affiliates!
- You create more valuable content for your own and other people's websites that the search engines can index - driving more traffic to your website.
- You create additional installments for your autoresponder series that you can easily turn into profitable "mini-courses."
- You'll get better and better at picking topics, distributing articles and your traffic logs will start to snowball with visitors.
- ... much more!

Let's get started...

Why Promoting With Articles Works Very Well!

We promise a lot in this book, but the overriding theme remains the same throughout the entire publication:

We'll teach you how to first write and polish an article to a professional level and then use it to attract high volumes of "targeted traffic" to your website.

You can generate thousands of targeted, money-making visitors through:

1. Free articles on your website people recommend to others
2. Ezines publishing your articles for their subscribers
3. Affiliates publishing articles marketing your website
4. Getting search engines to index your articles
5. Submitting your articles to article announcement sites
6. … Much more!

It's just like the Pied Piper leading people to visit your website — almost against their will — to buy your products and services.

I know at this point you're thinking, "Ok! Let's hear it. How do you do it? Don't give me that 1 o'clock in the morning 'infomercial' pitch! I know it all too well from late night television. No more generalities please! Can you produce what you say or not?"

Have no fear. Yes, we can and we will deliver!

We subscribe to the theory of business as a "pond" of water.

Imagine right now a "pond" of business activity with water (new business and customers) pouring into the pond at one end and water pouring out of the pond (customers leaving, business changes, email addresses go bad, etc.) at the other end. The movement never stops.

> **Your GOAL:** As a businessperson, you want to keep the pond water fresh, deep and free from stagnation. If the pond dries up you experience what we call "business failure!"

By the way, we've watched this "pond" model prove itself by watching everything from turnover at a huge shopping mall every five years when the store leases expired, to the turnover of subscribers in our own lists and autoresponders. No matter what business you find yourself engaged in, business constantly flows out of the pond and you must keep up and grow by constantly helping new business flow into your pond.

So how do you avoid having your pond go dry like a bone baking in the desert sun?

Simple. You do it by keeping a constant flow of three things into your business:

1. People
2. Products
3. Profits

Those three things apply to the largest and the smallest businesses — online or off. By revealing those three "P's" we just saved you the time spent reading a 1,000 page economics book to find out the same thing.

But what does this have to do with writing and promoting with articles?

Well, articles may just represent the "keys to the castle" when it comes to the Three "P's".

Here's why…

Since every other business also online needs their share of the 3 P's too, you, along with everyone else in the world, get hit with hundreds, even thousands, of business pitches daily. So many in fact that you probably glaze over and don't even notice the majority of them.

Think of all the advertising avenues fighting for your attention daily?

The list includes:

- Ads in the yellow pages
- Ads in Magazines
- Ads in Newspapers
- Direct mail circulars in your "snail" mailbox
- Radio pitches
- TV ads
- Store fronts in malls
- Bars and restaurants
- Highway billboards
- Illegal signs on stop signs & telephone poles
- Legitimate email messages
- Spam email or UCE (unsolicited commercial email)

The daily saturation nearly equals the air you breathe and gets more stifling with each passing day!

In response, everyone — especially people online — has a set of defenses built up against anything that resembles a "pitch" or a sales job. They have erected a psychological wall around themselves in order to feel protected against the bombardment of sales and marketing messages.

> **FACT:** If you want to sell anything to your prospects, you must first get behind their built-up defenses and connect with them on a deeper level than your competitors.

Connecting with them does NOT involve more frequent or more obnoxious advertising. It does not mean using "sneaky" tactics either. Tricking people into trusting you for the moment always backfires in the long run!

Establishing credibility for yourself and your company as THE trusted expert, while at the same time reducing people's fears, rates the FASTEST way to get behind any prospect's defenses and persuade them to buy. Do this and you will succeed!

Establish yourself as a trusted, credible expert and you stand miles above your competition in the hearts and minds of your customers and prospects.

But how do you do that?

How do you establish credibility while reducing people's fears in the process?

Well, ask yourself, what wins your attention and finally gets you to spend your money?

Have you ever really thought about what type of "hustle" or "pitch" will actually separate you from your money?

For most people, the reason they finally buy comes down to the fact that the seller got behind their "defenses" with information that made them trust the seller enough to buy. In other words, the seller built up enough credibility in the mind of the buyer to tip the scales in favor of making a purchase rather than not!

So how do you gain this credibility? Easy! Keep reading…

FACT: Publishing and promoting with free articles gives you one of the most powerful opportunities available to tip the buyer's credibility scale in your favor and BUY your product.

Why?

The answer lies no further than your local newspaper. Stop reading this ebook right now, go pick up a newspaper and come back.

Look at the newspaper and answer one simple question: Which information in the newspaper do you trust more – the news articles or the advertisements?

Don't read the newspaper? Then pick up a magazine and ask the same question: Which information in the magazine do you trust more – the articles or the advertisements?

For most people, the articles receive the overwhelming vote of confidence because people have been conditioned to think "they aren't trying to sell me anything." We, as a culture, have been conditioned since an early age to believe and *trust* what we read when it appears in a "news" or "information" format.

In short, if we see news or information in print – we believe it and we trust the author!

The great news comes when you realize that you can use this lifetime of conditioning to your advantage to sell more of your own products and services! Why? Because few things create as much trust and confidence in the minds of your prospects as reading an article you've written on a subject of specific and intense interest to them.

If you want to **establish credibility quickly** with your prospects and get behind their defenses against "advertising"...

If you want to **differentiate yourself** from your competition as THE trusted and respected "expert" in virtually any area you choose...

If you want to **build and solidify your relationship** with your existing customers so they'll buy from you again and again...

... then writing, publishing, and promoting your business with articles will prove itself as one of the **best** and most **cost-effective** strategies available... no matter what size business you operate!

Let us show you step-by-step exactly how to do it right now...

Part 1
Creating Your Article

In this first section we'll teach you from "A to Z" how to create a professional-quality article you can feel proud of. One that will help you not only generate traffic, but quickly establish you as an expert in the minds of your prospects in virtually any field you choose!

The Article Writing Process (Overview)

Let's take a look at a general over view of the writing process before getting down into specific details where we will teach the quick and easy article writing techniques you <u>never</u> learned in school.

First, we'll take a quick look at the big picture to familiarize you with the process then, we'll get you started with a fun and extremely valuable exercise to get your brain cells churning!

Step #1 - Target your audience.

Exactly which group of people do you want to reach? Identify exactly who will have the highest interest level in your article's content and its benefits for them.

Step #2 - Brainstorm extremely popular topics.

Think about your target audience. What problems do they have? What dreams do they have? What keeps them up late at night worried sick?

Step #3 - Decide in advance the outcome you want from your article.

Do you want people to visit your web site, click on your affiliate link, subscribe to your autoresponder, buy your product, or come back for a repeat purchase?

Step #4 - Make your subject irresistible to web visitors!

You do this one of three ways:

a. Promise a huge benefit (which you can deliver) — or

b. Arouse their curiosity to where they can't resist reading — or

c. Scare them half to death with a problem directly affecting them!

Step #5 - Outline the points you want to cover.

This part of the process will enlarge and also tighten your article without rambling over unnecessary topics.

Step #6 - Organize the points into a structure.

You organize your tools and building materials for a construction project to avoid a mess, so do the same with your words to avoid a collection of word gibberish.

Step #7 - Choose your voice or writing style.

Choose exactly how you want people to perceive you when they read your article and your call to action.

Step #8 – Write your article by fleshing out your outline.

Include the secondary topics or points of elaboration for your main points. Do you think a detective thriller author writes a 700-page mystery without making a plan of points for each chapter so it all comes together at the end?

Step #9 - Edit your article into a "lean, mean, attention-getting machine."

We all suffer from "run-on at the mouth" and editing takes care of this. Follow these steps to tighten your article into a compact, powerful information package.

Step #10 - Polishing your article.

Even after a thorough editing you'll want to look for any information you may have left out or any points you can clarify and streamline.

Step #11 - Ensure your article contains the three critical parts of any highly effective article.

Take a step back from your article to make sure it contains all 3 critical elements.

Now, let's do an exercise that will get your first article well under way in no time flat…

EXERCISE FOR THE ARTICLE WRITING PROCESS OVERVIEW:

Fill in the blanks for each question with just a few words on each point. For each question we have supplied an example of the actual thought process that went into an extremely popular article we published. At the end of the exercise we'll show you the actual article so you can see how all the parts come together.

1. **What do I know that makes me an expert compared to 80% of the people in the world?**

   ____

   Example: I know how to stop people from spamming me and filling my email box with junk mail and viruses.

   NOTE: If you immediately say to yourself, "I'm not an expert in anything!", then just ask yourself, "What would I like to know about which would make me an expert?"

2. **Who would want to know about what I know?**

   ____

   Example: Anybody who has gotten sick and tired of their email inbox filling up with spam or viruses.

3. **What do I want people to get from my knowledge?**

   ____

   Example: I want them to understand they can stand up against spam and fight back!

4. **How do I want them to respond to my article?**

   ____

   Example: I want them to sign up for my newsletter.

5. **What can I promise them if they read this article?**

   ____

Example: I want them to learn a surefire way to drastically reduce the amount of spam and viruses making it into their inboxes.

6. **The six main points (or 3, or 5, or 7) I can make from my knowledge on this topic?**

____

____

____

____

____

____

Example: Points to cover based on my expertise:

1. Show people how to prevent downloading viruses to their computer.
2. Give an example of an actual virus and how I stopped it.
3. Emphasize the importance of using anti-virus software.
4. Give a source for finding additional tools to stop viruses before they even get downloaded to your computer.
5. Give a specific example of how I found and used the program to stop viruses.
6. Give the side benefit of realizing I could stop downloading spam too!
7. Give people a strong reason to update their anti-virus software

7. **How do I communicate best in talking: formal, informal, funny, serious, laid back, up close and personal?**

____

Example: I communicate best when talking as a down-to-earth, no-nonsense, "just the facts" type of person.

8. **What sub-points or explanations do I want to include with my main points in #6 (above) to expand my article or emphasize a particular point?**

____

____

____

____

Example: Additional points to get across in my article:

1. Help people realize what a waste of time these viruses create.
2. Convey the serious vulnerability faced by anyone who uses Windows.
3. Show how easy the solution I found can make your life.
4. Tie the article into a recent virus outbreak that already has large numbers of people keenly interested in the topic and how to deal with the problem.

9. **What problems can people expect if they do not follow up on the information / advice contained in my article?**

____

Example: They'll waste time dealing with serious viruses, risk losing their valuable data, and continue to experience intense frustration with mountains of spam on a daily basis!

10. **What benefits can people expect to gain by reading my article?**

____

Example: Readers will arm themselves with an effective, free tool they can use to massively cut down on the dangerous viruses as well as annoying spam they download to their computers!

11. **What potential follow-up articles could I offer if this one hits a chord with readers?**

____

Example: Additional topics I could cover:

1. Additional tools to combat the viruses problem.
2. Resources for reporting and stopping spammers.

Congratulations!!! Believe it or not, by completing this exercise you have already completed a HUGE portion of the article writing process!

By compiling your thoughts in this manner you have formed the basis of your first article and maybe even a couple more! In fact, based on what you've just done, along with just a bit more instruction, you could write your first article right now!

I'm sure you can see with this book, you hold in your hands a very powerful tool for turning your ideas into well-organized, complete, POWERFUL articles, others will eagerly read.

With these tools you know you can write a great article and use it to build your business!

Before we move on to the next chapter, let me show you the actual article I wrote, that came from my doing the example exercise above. This article ranks as one of my most popular so far and has brought me a bonanza of website traffic and subscribers to my newsletter http://www.thenetreporter.com.

==================================

Stop Spam and Viruses at Same Time

by Jim Edwards http://www.thenetreporter.com

==================================

A recent virus outbreak caused no end of headaches for those infected as well as computer users who repeatedly received tainted emails. Though this virus didn't rate high for physical destruction, it did rate as one of the wildest and most criminally intent viruses ever.

"Bad Trans" reportedly logs actual keystrokes and then transmits credit card and password data it captures to the person who released it.

If that doesn't scare you enough, the old safety rule of "you have to open the attachment to get the virus" doesn't apply with this nasty little bug!

Anyone using Microsoft Outlook or Outlook Express runs the risk of infection if they use the preview pane—which most people do.

Virtually anyone with up-to-date anti-virus software found the virus relatively easy to stop before infecting their system, but they also found dealing with the virus highly inconvenient and a serious waste of time.

Every time an infected email arrived they had to stop and clean it up. Adding to the inconvenience - this latest virus carries a 40K attachment, no small file on a dial-up connection, especially if you get it emailed to you several times a day.

Quite frankly, I got extremely tired of downloading this virus, which seemed to come in wave after wave. Out of curiosity, I looked to see if I could find a program that would let me check my email before even downloading it through my regular email program, Outlook Express.

I went to the popular download site (www.download.com) and started looking around for free programs that would let me preview my email on my mail server without downloading the actual messages.

After some searching I discovered a program called "Mail Washer" (www.mailwasher.net), a free program that allows you to check the headers in your email box before downloading to your computer. You can see who sent the email, the subject line (a big spam tip-off), the size of the email message along with any attachments, and the date.

Now this solution won't apply in every instance (no solution ever does) but it really helped me out this time. Every version of the virus I saw carried two easily identifiable characteristics - an re: in the usually blank subject line and an underscore (_) in front of the return email address. With this program I could immediately spot the virus and eliminate it with a simple mouse click.

However, I noticed an excellent side benefit! I also eliminated the vast majority of unsolicited email bombarding my computer daily. Rather than wait for dozens of messages to download, I just click "delete" next to the offending message subjects and eliminate those too without downloading the messages. What a time saver!

This last wave of viruses should teach all of us that prevention and preparation hold the key to keeping our online sanity. Make sure to keep your anti-virus program updated weekly and consider checking your email before it ever downloads to your computer.

Furthermore, expect viruses to get more sophisticated and more destructive, and you must make it your responsibility to protect your computer, your data, and personal information against loss.

Jim Edwards writes a syndicated newspaper column helping non-technical people understand and use the Internet better!

Get the best online news, tips, tricks & more FREE by email!

Click Here Now => http://www.TheNetReporter.com

==============================

Why are some people getting rich selling their ebooks?

Jim Edwards & Joe Vitale have created the *ultimate* guide: "How to Write and Publish your own Outrageously Profitable eBook... in as little as 7 Days!"

FREE Details: ==> http://www.7dayebook.com

FREE Email-Course: ==> mailto:7dayebook@getresponse.com

==============================

Why people will read your articles!

Let us ask you a question: **Why do <u>you</u> want to write an article?** Simple! 99% of the time you want to use it to get more visitors to your site. More visitors in front of your online store window means more people will buy. Stated bluntly, <u>money</u> translates into your main reason for increasing web site visitors.

Now that we know *your* motivation, let's talk about what the readers want, because giving them what they want translates quickly and easily into your getting what you want!

Why would any potential customers want to read an article written by you?

Well, it comes down to about a half a dozen different reasons we'll boil down for you right here. These particular motivations do NOT appear in any particular order of importance, each rates just as useful as the next based on the needs of your target audience.

1. **The article addresses a technical problem they really want to overcome or avoid.**

   Example: How to speed up your PC without expensive upgrades.

2. **The article offers a solution to a problem currently costing them money.**

   Example: How to slash your newspaper advertising costs by 65% while doubling your conversion rate.

3. **It offers a time saving solution that translates into more money earned or saved per hour/day/week.**

   Example: How SPAM costs you at least $50 a day in time… and what to do about it.

4. **It addresses a problem of personal concern or stress, not necessarily measured in money.**

   Example: How to find 1-2 extra hours of free time to spend each day with your family by reducing your time spent dealing with customer service issues by 75%.

5. **It presents an expertise or advice which they find useful immediately or in the future.**

   Example: Six ways to immediately increase the effectiveness of your sales copy or brochure in under 5 minutes.

6. **It offers the promise of immediate fun, amusement or entertainment.**

   Example: 3 offbeat ways to entertain your kids for hours on a rainy day with items you already have around the house.

Other motivations may arise for your particular audience, however you can trace the origins of most successful articles back to these six (6) reasons they read. Start thinking about how you could use each of these motivations as the subject for an article that really speaks to the needs of your target audience.

If any good ideas come to you at this point (or any other as you go through this ebook) make sure you write them down immediately!

Now, let's get down to Step #1, "Targeting Your Audience"…

Step 1 - Targeting your audience for maximum impact!

Two key questions you must answer when targeting your audience:

1. **Question: What group do you want to reach with your article?**

   What do they look like... talk like... sound like... love.... hate.... desire more than anything else in the whole world right now?

   Examples:

   a. Homeowners who want to sell their house and save the commission.

   b. People who operate online businesses and want to earn increased affiliate commissions.

   c. Dentists who want to attract more business to their practice.

   d. Florists who want to sell more flowers by learning how to creatively arrange baskets.

   e. Single females between the ages of 18 and 27 who want to find eligible men to marry.

2. **Question: What will people want from <u>you</u> after they read your article?**

   If you do your job correctly and create a compelling article that makes people sit up and take notice... what represents the next logical step for them after reading it?

Example:

a. Request more information that builds upon the issues raised in your article so they can take more action on their own.

b. Request a referral to a person or thing (software, website) that will solve their problem or accomplish a result for them without much effort on their part.

c. Investigate additional resources (websites, articles, mini-courses) that expand on the subject of your article.

d. Take some other action or request information as appropriate based on your target audience and the subject of your article.

To answer these two questions you must first figure out the profile of your target audience.

Can you narrow down the characteristics of your audience by:

- **age range**: young, old, middle aged
- **gender**: male or female or both
- **geographic location**: U.S., Europe, other
- **level of income**: high, low, doesn't matter
- **technical ability**: Newbies, computer programmers, somewhere in between
- **social or political interests**: conservative, liberal, middle of the road
- **degree of involvement with the web**: own a website, barely have email
- **job relationship to web**: use web for work daily, weekly, rarely
- **owners of specific software or hardware**: PC users, Mac users, Windows
- **users of a specific type of service**: website hosting, DSL / Cable access, shopping carts, credit card processing
- **physical characteristics**: active, couch potato

You must create a clear picture in your mind of the type of person you will speak to in your article. Though your articles will get read by hundreds and thousands of people, it will get read **one person at a time**. Make sure you speak directly to each member of your audience by getting a clear picture of the ideal person in your audience.

The main outcomes or purposes <u>**you**</u> want from your articles include:

1. **Recognition as an expert in your field.**

   Your article will clearly demonstrate any such expertise simply from its brevity and completeness

2. **Additions to your subscriber list.**

   More people on your list will lead to hard cash sales for your product.

3. **People to buy from you!**

   You want people to buy your ebook, info-product, physical product or service now… *and* in the future.

In order to accomplish one or more of these goals you MUST first target your readers and decide exactly which group of people you want to reach and describe them in enough detail that you can easily envision a typical member of that audience sitting in front of you.

No wrong or right answer exists, only good, better and best descriptions for you to work with as you create your ideal subscriber in your mind.

Look at this example of audience targeting:

Good Description: Men who like to knit socks.

Better Description: Men who drive trucks who like to knit socks.

Best Description: Lonely truck driving men who like to knit socks at rest stops in the middle of the night while drinking stale coffee and listening to country music.

Now that might actually represent a silly example, but do you see how getting more descriptive creates a clearer picture of your audience members? The clearer your description – the better you can speak straight into their brains!

EXERCISE FOR STEP #1 – TARGETING YOUR AUDIENCE:

In one sentence, write out whom you want to target with your article:

____

____

____

____

Step 2 - Brainstorming Article Topics.

How to get an idea for a great article that people will drop everything to read.

Keep these general hints in mind when starting on a brainstorming session and it will help you come up with a "killer" article idea.

Try to brainstorm article ideas that will affect people in your target audience the following ways:

1. Look for ideas that will excite people about the subject because they never thought of it that way before and they need to follow through with your article to find satisfaction / closure / avoid harm.

   Examples:

   a. Offbeat ways to improve your garage sale profits
   b. 12 words to use in your descriptions to double online auction responses
   c. How to stop spam and viruses at the same time

2. Ideas or subjects that heighten existing concerns because of technical problems or the actions of unscrupulous people make good articles.

   Examples:

a. What your _______ isn't telling you about _______ that can ________! (fill in the blanks)

   i. What your web host isn't telling you about bandwidth charges that can bite you on the tail once you start rolling in the traffic!

b. How to avoid ________________ because of ____________.

   i. How to avoid having your website shut down because of spam complaints arising as a result of spammers "relaying" email through your website's email servers.

An excellent article subject will often put a "new twist" on an existing idea or problem. People love a new spin on an old idea.

Example subjects:

"Accept Credit Cards Online Without Monthly Fees Or Long-Term Obligations"

"12 Money-Making Uses for Your Old Computer"

"Christmas Shoppers Say 'Byte Me' This Year"

Important Note: Great article ideas fully explain a specific part of the overall picture, but also leave room for additional information later.

Let us state that differently, just to make sure you understand it.

Your article should represent a juicy piece of a larger steak. Give them a bite of the best steak in the world (your article) and use that bite to entice them to get the whole steak (buy your ebook, buy through an affiliate link, sign up for your newsletter, etc.)

Remember your favorite TV series and adventure books where the hero dispatched a particular villain, but you knew another one lurked around the corner to cause more problems next week on TV or in the next book. Use your articles the same way. Build excitement and anticipation so people WANT to get more!

Specific brainstorming suggestions for coming up with an idea for your next "Killer Article."

1. **Brainstorm Technique - Solve a problem for people**, either in:

   a. one bite-sized article, which solves an entire problem, or,

   b. solves part of a problem and then uses the resource box to drive them to the rest of the solution.

I used such an approach in ROTC in school. I would shine one shoe for someone before an inspection to a very high gloss. I charged nothing for this service, however if they wanted the other one shined to the same gloss, then I charged as much for one as for two. Don't count that tactic as bait and switch but rather as "tease and produce." Your article can do the same thing – just don't make them angry in the process.

Solve one complete part of the overall problem and then show them how they can solve the bigger problem with the solution you offer for a price or by taking action on their part (sign up for your newsletter).

Examples:

- An article about 5 tips for getting your house ready for sale would lead to an ebook on selling your house yourself without an agent.
- An article about increasing the effectiveness of your headlines would lead to an online course about writing effective sales copy.
- An article about skin care would lead to a website selling vitamin enriched facial moisturizer.
- An article about how to negotiate the best interest rate on a mortgage might lead to a website for a mortgage company or to an ebook that taught people every aspect of the mortgage shopping process.

2. **Brainstorm Technique - Address breaking news**, especially if it impacts your audience directly *and they don't even realize it yet.*

That gives an advantage to you for playing the part of "first alert" and shows a true interest and concern for your readers as well as demonstrating that you "keep on top of things."

A genuine "public service" type article that selflessly solves a problem for people will bring them to your site much more open minded about the worth of your expertise to help them.

3. **Brainstorm Technique - Address changes in general / industry changes / technology changes.**

Show people how changes will affect them now and also how it will likely affect them in the future. If it directly affects their pocket books in the short run, their attitude of resentment will not direct itself towards you since they realize you didn't cause it. Rather, you warned them and can help, so why not buy your product / services!

We all know the old cliché about the messenger who bears bad news, he usually gets shot but, in this case, if you handle the news from a removed but informative position which doesn't get in their faces, you will benefit from the bad news or significant changes.

4. **Brainstorm Technique – Questions posted in "forums" and on "discussion boards."**

Don't underestimate the potential of this source. Don't think that because everyone asks the same thing over and over that someone already solved the problems. Your approach and answers might provide the breakthrough, which would help the majority of people experiencing the same problems.

Take a close look at the questions people ask in forums and see if you can spot trends or continued trouble spots, which your expertise can solve through a single or series of articles.

Also, the "good old" frequently asked questions (FAQ) page present on many websites also holds good potential for a series of articles.

5. **Brainstorm Technique - Use other people's articles as a springboard or reference point** for your own take on the same subject or problem.

You can expand on what they already wrote on the subject. It also allows you to take the same topic and put your own spin, on it. If you don't believe this then take a look for a week sometime at the editorial pages of a large newspaper. See how many different spins and solutions you can find on the same topic of war or peace in whatever region around the world. How about the number of solutions to continuing economic problems in this country or the sad state of education in whatever area of subject matter at whatever level or geographical region of the country.

Ten different voices will hold eleven different solutions. So don't feel reluctant to speak out on something which already stirred up dissent or concern. You just might find the right balance to gain thousands of website visitors in the process.

6. **Brainstorm Technique - Questions people email you as a matter of course.**

If you've been on the Internet for more than a couple of months with an online business, chances rate quite high that someone has emailed you a question or two. Look at those questions for article ideas that will have a special and immediate relevance to your particular audience. Our own experience has taught us that for every question you get, 20 to 100 other people have the same question but, for whatever reason, haven't asked you.

Using these six general areas and methods will enable you to brainstorm topics articles as long as the subject holds any interest for you. Truth and justice, good and evil never run short of topics for discussion and neither will the problems faced by your target audience.

If you ever run into a brick wall for article ideas, go to your target audience and simply ask them this question:

"What is the #1 question on your mind about ______________?"

Fill in the blank with your specific area of interest. Examples:

- What is the #1 question on your mind about ebook marketing?

- What is the #1 question on your mind about selling your house yourself without an agent?
- What is the #1 question on your mind about getting more visitors to your "brick & mortar" floral shop?
- What is the #1 question on your mind about improving your relationship with your kids / co-workers / in-laws?

EXERCISE FOR STEP #2 - BRAINSTORMING TOPICS.

Fill in each blank as best you can. A little "brain sweat" here will yield big results in your traffic logs when you launch a successful article.

As you go through each one you'll start to see a pattern or a high level of interest on your part in a particular subject area. In other words – the lights will go onand you'll "know" the topic of the article you want to write.

- I want to help people with their problems in the following areas:

  ____
  ____
  ____
  ____

- Solving problems in those areas would then lead to further articles and solutions in follow-up areas, including:

  ____
  ____
  ____
  ____

- Breaking news / current events affecting people who could benefit from my area of expertise include the following areas or subjects:

  ____
  ____
  ____
  ____

- Recent industry, general and technology changes, which can or will affect my target audience include the following:

  ____
  ____
  ____
  ____

- Those changes will affect them right now as follows:

  ____

  ____

- Those changes will affect them in the future as follows:

  ____

  ____

- The five most frequently asked questions I see, from people in my target audience, either emailed to me or posted in forums & discussion groups include:

  1. ____
  2. ____
  3. ____
  4. ____
  5. ____

- Two recent articles by others which I can use as a springboard for my articles include:

  ____

  ____

  - How can I take a different view on the same issues in each article?

    ____

    ____

  - How can I expand on what they've already written?

    ____

    ____

  - How can I take the same topic in both articles and put my own spin on the critical areas of each article?

    ____

    ____

Now choose your topic for your article and write it clearly here as a statement of your intention!

Example:

> I will write an article explaining to my target audience how they can accept credit cards on their websites without a credit check, no minimum monthly fees, no long-term contracts, and without purchasing any equipment.

____

____

____

____

____

Step 3 – Decide Your Outcome For Your Article In Advance

So far you've targeted your audience and come up with a specific topic for your article which you wrote down in the last section. Now, in this section, we'll quickly analyze what you want to accomplish with your article so you reach your goals.

Forget everything you learned in English class in school because it doesn't have anything to do with what you want to accomplish here. You don't want to please Miss Smith, the teacher, who made certain that you crossed every "t" and dotted every "i." You want to please the thousands of people who can read your article and visit your site or sign up for your newsletter.

You also want your article to portray a high degree of expertise so your readers show up at your site or take the action you want, because they trust you and your advice.

For the most part, with every article you publish you want readers to take one or more of the following concrete action steps:

- You want people to read your article and click the **web link** in your resource box, which will:
    - Deliver them to your website so they can:
        - Read your sales letter and buy your product(s)
        - Read your sales letter and hire you for your services

        - Sign up for your newsletter, mini-course or autoresponder
    - Take them to someone else's website through your affiliate link where you earn commissions if they buy.
- You want people to read your article and click an **email link** in your resource box, which will send an email to you to:
    - Get more information or open other lines of communication
    - Subscribe to a newsletter or mini-course

Besides taking the action step of either clicking on a web link or sending an email, you also want to have a specific psychological or mental impact on your readers. With every article you write, you want to encourage readers to see you as an expert in the field of your choosing. By doing so you will build credibility for future articles on similar and related topics you write later.

EXERCISE FOR STEP #3 – YOUR OUTCOME

State exactly what action you want people to take as a result of reading your article.

Example:

> As a result of reading my article, I want members of my target audience to get excited enough to click the link to my website to get more information about my ebook, because it solves a specific problem they have.

Write down the outcome you want from your article now:

____

____

____

____

____

____

____

Well done!

You now know **whom** you want to write for (target audience), **what** you want to write about (subject), and the action(s) you want them to take as a result of reading your article.

Now let's write your hard charging, irresistible, avalanche-of-website-traffic-generating article!

Step 4 - How to Make Your Article Subject Irresistible.

Very few people pick up a newspaper and read it front to back, page by page until they finish. Rather they skip around and read whatever appeals to them, similar to picking out certain items from the salad bar in a restaurant.

So what tickles your palate and your reading eye from all the printed words in a newspaper or magazine?

Three general but very strong attractors will usually do the trick to pull your readers into your article.

Attractor #1 - Making a huge promise of tantalizing benefits.

> "Don't pass up this amazing offer which will save you thousands of dollars over the next few years on your heating, plumbing, food, or medical bills!"

That will usually get everyone's attention long enough to read until they decide that someone wants to lighten your wallet with the "too good to be true" deal!

So what can you do to succeed with your article, which promises huge benefits, when people automatically turn off when they hear or see these never ending pitches?

You want your article, which promises that huge benefit, to whisper gently but firmly in the target audience's ear and make them want to drop everything and start reading.

You do this with a headline that sums up the main benefit(s) your target audience wants more than anything else in the world when it comes down to the subject you write about... but you still keep that promise within the general realm of believability!

Examples of headlines with tantalizing benefits:

1. 3 Quick, Non-Violent Ways to Train Your Dog To Stop Soiling The Furniture
2. Quickly Lose 20 Pounds Naturally and Without Dieting
3. How To Double Your Stock Market Profits – Even in a Downward Economy
4. How to Improve Your Love Life in 3 Easy Steps

Attractor #2 - Invoke Strong Curiosity

Creating a strong feeling of curiosity within members of your target audience will often cause people to take the next step, which means reading your article!

But Beware: The built-in skepticism and suspicion in our world today will make them also "pitch your pitch" at the slightest sign of deceit or manipulation. Many an online marketer has abused this powerful attractor only to get burned in the end by subscribers who felt used by their manipulative "tactics."

The tabloid newspapers at the checkout lines do a great job of teasing with the front page headlines to get you to buy for the information inside. When the headline says that the world-class beauty queen finally revealed to her billionaire husband, her true love in her bed on the yacht, don't buy the paper to find out that he peeked into her bedroom and saw a poodle lounging on his pillow. That leaves readers feeling cheated.

However, we all watch and listen intently when watching the news and the consumer reporter comes on to tell you why the latest and hottest toy for Christmas can actually cause harm, death and destruction if used incorrectly.

So when you invoke a strong curiosity with your article, make certain you keep on the safe side of truth and don't cross over into "you gotta be kiddin me". Your readers won't give you a second chance if you turn them off the first time by falling outside the realm of believability.

Often the best way to invoke curiosity in your headline involves asking a question or making what seems like an odd statement.

Examples of "curiosity" headlines:

1. Which of These Website Design Mistakes Will You Make?
2. An Offbeat Way To Cut Your Car Repairs By $500 a Year – Without Marrying a Mechanic!
3. A 300 Year Old Folk-Remedy Relieves Back Pain Overnight – Without Drugs!

3. Scare the "Bejabbers" out of them!

FACT: Scaring someone half to death will also draw readers to your article. But, as in balancing a strong curiosity attractor against nonsense, you need to couch your article in terms that alert the reader to the problem, but also offers a quick response or alternative solution to the major problem you bring to their attention.

"Martians land in New Jersey," the line from the old radio program in the 1930's caused a lot of problems because it provided no solution to the panic it created. Your approach with a serious problem should follow the method used to alert people in a crowded theater to the danger of fire, without just yelling "fire." Tell them in a calm voice where and how to walk safely to the exits.

Your article should contain the same elements of direction to avoid the flames you just brought to their attention.

Examples of "scary" headlines:

1. Is There A Hacker Inside Your Computer? (Very popular article)
2. Avoid Web Hosting Con Artists
3. Defeat Affiliate Link "Hijackers"
4. Prevent Online Identity Theft

Regardless of which type of attractor you choose to use, your headline serves as the pitchman, much like a carnival barker, who stands on the soap box and tries to get people to come in to see the show. Your headline's main job: getting people to stop their current activity and start reading your article.

Think about what you want to convey to people and, if necessary, write out many sentences and start paring them down until a single sentence tells it all. Remember the various slogans for ads which caught your attention: "Things go better with Coke" or "Sooner or later you'll own General" or "Ford gives you better ideas" or "Ask the man who owns one".

Think of the ads or commercials which have stuck in your mind and ask yourself, "How could I describe my idea or service in the ad format, or the attention getting way?"

Brainstorm your own irresistible article headline using the following examples for guidance.

1. **The TOP TEN Reasons ________________________ and What To Do About It**

   Examples using this formula:

   a. The TOP TEN Reasons People Fail Online and What To Do About It

   b. The TOP TEN Reasons Most Marriages Fail and What To Do About It

   c. The TOP TEN Reasons Employees Quit and What To Do About It

   d. The TOP TEN Reasons The IRS Audits Your Tax Returns and What To Do About It

2. **A Simple Solution For ________________**

a. A Simple Solution For Stopping Telemarketers Cold

b. A Simple Solution For Getting More Website Traffic

c. A Simple Solution For Curing Athlete's Foot

3. ______ Surefire Ways To ____________ While ____________

a. Four Surefire Ways To Get More Website Traffic While Decreasing Advertising Costs

b. Two Surefire Ways To Build Your Business While Spending More Time With Your Family

c. Three Surefire Ways To Reduce Stress While Increasing Your Happiness and Well-being

d. Five Surefire Ways To Live Like a Millionaire While Making An Hourly Wage

Other article headline templates:

STOP ________ Nearly 100% Of The Time
STOP Hackers Nearly 100% Of the Time

Avoid ________________ By ________________
Avoid "Downsizing" By Making Yourself Too Important To Fire!

Stop __________ In __________ Using ___________
Stop Smoking In Three Days Using Common, Everyday Herbs

Don't Get Caught Short _____________
Don't Get Caught Short At Tax Time

Increase Your ________ In _________
Increase Your Website Traffic In 5 Short Days

EXERCISE FOR STEP #4 – MAKE YOUR ARTICLE SUBJECT IRRESISTIBLE

If you still haven't written down a headline that summarizes a very attractive reason to read your article, let's quickly go through these steps.

1. Based on the subject or topic you chose in Step #2, write three statements, premises, or headlines which promise strong benefits to the reader.

   a. ______________________________

   b. ______________________________

   c. ______________________________

2. Based on the subject or topic you chose in Step #2, write three statements, which will arouse curiosity for potential readers who belong to your target audience.

   a. ______________________________

   b. ______________________________

   c. ______________________________

3. Based on the subject or topic you chose in Step #2, write three statements you could write an article about, which would scare the "Bejabbers" off people if they knew of them.

   a. ______________________________

   b. ______________________________

   c. ______________________________

4. Based on what you've written above, create or choose three absolutely irresistible headlines right now. They will form the basis for your first articles after reading this book.

   a. ____

   b. ____

   c. ____

Now, let's move on to actually creating your "killer" article…

Step 5 – Outline the Points You Want to Cover

The next step in the article writing process actually rates rather simple. Take some quiet time and write down all the points you want to cover in your article.

This includes any ideas, any quotes, any websites, and anything at all you think should go into your article. Call this a grocery list, checklist or "catchall" for materials on a building site.

The idea here: don't forget anything in case you want to use it and not forget later in the heat of composing the article. You can always discard later, but you might forget to include something, if you don't jot down all the points you can think of in advance.

Some things to consider as you create the main points for your article:

- Do you want to provide general information for readers, answer a question on a specific topic, or remedy a general problem affecting many people?

  If so, then you'll need to make sure you cover the topic or problem from beginning to end. If the problem or subject requires more than 500-800 words to cover, then you'll need to narrow it down to a specific part of the overall problem, which you can cover in that amount of space.

- Do you want the first article to lead towards further articles in the same vein?

Often you'll think of an idea for your next article before you finish the one you currently have in progress. You can often build an audience's anticipation level for your next article simply by ending the current one with something like "Next time we'll cover ___________ so you can ____________."

- Keep the article simple in your use of language.

  You can read book reviews in the newspaper, but by the time you finish you don't know what the reviewer meant, other than to show that he or she could use big words and wrap them around confusing facts.

- "Short and simple" gets the point across. Look at examples such as "Halt," "Stop" or a favorite from cowboy movies which everyone knows, "Stampede".

  Let your article take the same approach with the opening sentence letting everyone know what you want to discuss. Say what you wish to discuss straight out. i.e. "The lousy job done in schools by teachers." "The disrespect shown to adults by children." or "The poor job done by service organizations for charitable work."

You get the idea! Look for points that can inflame or cause instant discussion, such as politics, religion, money and sex, then couch your opening article sentence in a way which stirs up the readers.

EXERCISE FOR STEP #5 – OUTLINE THE POINTS YOU WANT TO COVER

1. **Write down the main topic or concern which will serve as the subject of your article:**

   ___

   ___

   ___

   - Example: Have you been transmitting sensitive data such as passwords, credit card number and checking account information to a hacker without realizing it?

2. **Write down the five main points which make up the thrust of your article**

   1. ___
   2. ___
   3. ___
   4. ___
   5. ___

   Example:

   1. Tell them exactly what dangers exist.
   2. Impress upon people how important your firewall and anti-virus software really are.
   3. Tell people the consequences of having their ISP shut them down – make them feel the pain.
   4. Tell the story of what happened when my friend got infected with a Trojan horse – make it dramatic.
   5. Tell the readers how to prevent this from happening to them.

3. **Write down any quotes or references which apply to your article:**

    ____

    ____

    ____

    - Example: I should try to get a quote from a leading expert on network security. I should definitely include a link to a website where people can test their vulnerability to a hacker gaining entrance to their system.

4. **Write down any and all additional points which you should include in the article** (don't worry about putting them in the correct order at this point).

    ____

    ____

5. **Write down the conclusion your article should lead people to after reading it.** This can represent an action you want them to take (secure their computer against hackers), an opinion you want them to adopt (all hackers are scum), or even just to acknowledge the topic in the first place ("Wow, I didn't realize how vulnerable my computer actually is! I need to take action now.")

    ____

    ____

    ____

Step 6 – Organize Your Article Points Into A Structure

In this section we'll group and expand your points into the structure of your article. Follow the "**KISS**" approach for structuring your article…

Keep It Short and Simple!

By short we mean a few hundred words instead of a few thousand, which will force you to shave out all of the nonsense or extra fluff. Get to the point or your readers' attention span will wander all the way over to someone else's web site!

The price wars you saw at gas stations years ago reflected a simple way to get business, "Cheaper gas got the business for the same product." Customers saw no difference in octane rating, etc. only the price on the signs. Consider your article length as something which will get the visitors to fill up at your site instead of the web site across the street.

They want to know the price, not the history of gasoline from the first Pennsylvania oil well drilled in 1858.

Imagine your article like a river with a riverbank on either side. See the introduction to your article as the bank where your readers stand now. See the points of your article as a line of stepping stones over to the other riverbank. Imagine the conclusion of your article as the riverbank on the other side where you want your readers to finish.

In other words, start your article with an introduction of the main topic and lead people step by step to the conclusion you want them to draw from your article.

Now, let's quickly organize your points from the last section into the structure of your article (At this point we still have not written the article – that's coming up in a few minutes)…

EXERCISE FOR STEP #6 – ORGANIZE YOUR POINTS INTO A STRUCTURE

1. **Write out the introductory thought you want to introduce with your article.** Feel free to write out the exact sentence or paragraph you plan to use in the actual article. If you want you can simply use the same statement you used in the last section (Step #5) or you can restate it here for more clarity:

   ____

   ____

   Example: Imagine trying to access your email only to discover your Internet access cancelled because someone remotely controlled your computer and tried to hack into a government mainframe network. What a nightmare!

2. **Arrange the points of your article in the step-by-step order you will cover them.**

   1. ____
   2. ____
   3. ____
   4. ____
   5. ____

   Example or points organized in order:

   a. Tell the story of what happened when my friend got infected with a Trojan horse – make it dramatic!

   b. Tell people the consequences of having their ISP shut them down – make them feel the pain.

   c. Tell them exactly what dangers exist.

   d. Tell them why, how and where to test their computer for vulnerability.

e. Impress upon people how important your firewall and anti-virus software really rate.

f. Tell them how and where to find resources to prevent this from happening to them.

3. **Write out the concluding thought you want people to leave your article with, when they finish reading.** Feel free to write out the exact sentence or paragraph you plan to use in the actual article. If you want you can simply use the same statement you used in the last section (Step #5) or you can restate it here for more clarity:

 ____

 ____

 ____

 Example: Go get yourself a good firewall and an anti-virus program. Everyone on the net needs these two tools and you should consider yourself totally irresponsible if you don't have them and keep them up-to-date.

Congratulations! You've gone over the halfway point in writing your article; the rest will go very quickly from here. You can see at this point that so far you organized your thoughts into a simple, logical order and have the makings of a VERY powerful article.

How exciting!

By the way, while writing this section you just read, we only this minute got the following email message from an ezine publisher:

Hello,

I am sending a courtesy copy of my ezine.

I have included your informative article in it.

Many thanks,

Barbara

In This Issue:

Introduction

1.	Feature Article	A Hacker Inside your Computer
2.	Featured Friend	Stupidman
3.	Interesting Tidbit	What goes around comes around
4.	Classified Ads	

---

1. FEATURE ARTICLE

A Hacker Inside Your Computer?

- by Jim Edwards

http://www.TheNetReporter.com
(c) Jim Edwards - All Rights reserved
-=-=-=-=-=-=-=-=-=-=-=-=-=-=-=-=-=-

Imagine this nightmare scenario...

Side Note: She left my resource box intact and didn't add her affiliate link. Any sales as a result of this article come to me 100%!

Now, let's move on to the next section where you'll choose the "voice" you use to communicate to your readers…

Step 7 - Choose Your Voice or Writing Style.

After brainstorming your topic, jotting down and organizing the points of your article — and before you start writing — you must decide on the flavor or tone you will take with your audience.

Will you come out with a humorous or serious, simple or complicated, short or long or laid-back approach?

In other words… how will you "talk" to your readers?

To answer that question you need look no further than yourself!

How do you want someone to treat you? What attracts you to a certain person's writing style over another?

You'll speak differently to a grade school history class from the way you would to a group of adults operating small businesses from home on a part time basis.

Pull out the mental picture you made of the ideal member of your target audience back in Step #1 of the Article Writing Process. Think about the best voice or style you could use to communicate with that person and make them feel the most comfortable and receptive to your message.

In other words, though you may cover a topic common to many groups, you must tailor the style and delivery of your message to that ideal member of your target audience specifically.

Examples of different target audiences and voice approaches you could take for the same subject:

General Subject = Real Estate

1. **Lumberjacks: simple / short**

   Example Headline: "Loggers Lose Homes After Losing Jobs During Drought"

   Style or "Voice": Use short sentences. Relate everything back to them as rugged, hard-working individuals. Don't talk down to them.

2. **Weather forecasters: long / complicated**

   Example Headline: "El Nino Cycles Cause Confusion For New Home Starts In Coastal And Mountain Areas Of Country"

   Style or "Voice": Go into a lot of detail and use the words they use in the course of their business.

3. **Grade school teachers: serious / short**

   Example Headline: "New Loan Package Allows Teachers To Buy With 'Zero' Money Down"

   Style or "Voice": Watch your use of grammar and punctuation. They will judge the quality of your message delivery as much as the message itself.

4. **Retired farmers: laid back**

   Example Headline: "5 Ways To Increase Your Farm's Value Without Lifting A Finger"

   Style or "Voice": Keep your style relaxed and easy-going.

5. **Comedy show writers: short / fast-paced**

   Example Headline: "Rising Cost Of Housing No Laughing Matter"

   Style or "Voice": Keep the information moving in bite-sized chunks or "nuggets." Make short, strong statements that keep the information moving.

Golden Rule for Style or "Voice": No matter which style you choose, keep it simple without the fifty-cent words. Smart people already know all the words, so you won't impress them by using big ones.

How do you want people to perceive you?

Before answering this, think about your own personality. How do you interact with people? Would you fall under the category of:

- Serious
- Fun
- Approachable
- Coach / lecturer
- Authority figure

Really think about this for a minute.

What type of person do you think of when "serious" comes to mind? Doctors, lawyers, accountants, and other professional types who deal with the public's problems on a daily basis.

Who fits the category of a "fun" person?

Comedy club performers come to mind, but so do circus clowns.

What kind of humor turns you on? The fall down, slapstick, overdone type or the low-key statements which "zing" when you think about them for a minute.

We personally prefer the low-key types who tell about putting their humidifier and dehumidifier into the same room, locking the door and letting them fight it out!

The comics who dwell on basic human nature in daily living also rate quite highly with us and, if you'll notice, most of the people in their audiences. Get in your face comedy tends to turn off most people. That pretty much died off after vaudeville and silent movies.

So we recommend if you want to take a comic vein, write in the understated approach and let people get your point through low-key humor. It really does work better than funny faces and horn tooter noises.

What if you want to take a more approachable "coach" type of style? Who comes to mind?

Teachers, counselors, your parents, relatives, receptionists, nurses and other caregivers etc. They all carry an image that says, "I won't bite you if you want to talk to me."

Of the five categories of "persona" just listed, we would tend to want people to view us as approachable, not way off in some "Ivory Tower."

We all remember our school coaches, the special positions they held, and how we viewed them. They ranged all the way from the person you wanted to keep as a friend for life, to the drill sergeant type, who only wanted to toughen you up for the sport or life in general.

I really can't see too much benefit in projecting a, "winning is the only thing in life" attitude to your audience for most subjects you'll cover in articles, unless you specialize in giving winning tips for steel cage combat.

So if you see yourself as a coach/lecturer, then make sure your persona appeals to the widest spectrum of readers / website visitors who make up your target audience. Though we highly encourage you to find a niche target audience, make sure you don't back yourself into a tiny corner without enough of an audience to accomplish your business objectives.

By the way, think it through very carefully before placing yourself in the "authority figure" category for an article writing persona. This persona usually doesn't engender a warm and fuzzy feeling like going to your favorite uncle for advice.

Also, anyone who holds themselves up as "THE" unquestionable expert, usually spends more time defending themselves against people throwing tomatoes from the cheap seats in the balcony, than actually helping anyone in the audience.

So once you decide on the correct style or "voice" for you, how do you carry it over into writing your article?

You do it more easily and effortlessly than you might ever imagine…

Simple really! When you first get started writing articles, observe and think about how you talk to other people.

When you explain things to others what sort of tone do you use? Sharp? Friendly? Casual?

How do you explain yourself? Quickly? Long, drawn out?

Do you throw in bits of humor to emphasize the important points as you make them or do you rely strictly on the "facts" to back you up?

The easiest place to start finding your natural style or "voice" lies within the natural ways you've developed for communicating with people. Start with this because it represents your most "honest" way of communicating… and your readers love an honest, from-the-heart, genuine communicator above all else!

EXERCISE FOR STEP #7 – CHOOSE YOUR VOICE OR WRITING STYLE

Write out a brief statement of the voice you'll use to deliver your articles and make your individual mark on the minds of your readers.

____

____

____

Example:

I want my writing style to project the image of an approachable, yet extremely knowledgeable person who provides valuable information in a way that members of my target audience can use and benefit from immediately.

Step 8 – Write Your Article By Fleshing Out Your Outline

After thinking out what you want to say, outlining the points you want to cover, and deciding on the "voice" you want to use… you must now actually write the article!

Getting started rates as easy as opening your mouth to speak to a relative, co-worker or close friend. Just write the way you would talk. Use a straightforward tone without fooling around, getting wordy, or trying to impress people with your vocabulary.

You wouldn't say to someone, "It would give me the greatest of satisfaction if you would allow me to assist you at the present time". You would simply say, "May I help you?"

So you probably want to know how we will do this simple straightforward creation of sentences which flow so smoothly that no one can resist their message?

Quite simple really…

You should take a stand on something in your articles and not waver or act wishy-washy, because people would respect you for your position and your confidence. So write about each point with assurance that your information helps people understand your position and enables them to come to the same conclusions or take the actions you want.

TIP: If you get stuck, it often helps to pretend to write a letter to a friend. Use the outline you created in Section #6 to cover each point in the "letter" by fleshing it out with a few sentences that explain each point.

To illustrate this, let's dissect the article we outlined back in Section #6 and show the actual content created for a real article that has already run in front of thousands of people online.

Example opening idea from Section #6:

Imagine trying to access your email only to discover your Internet access cancelled because someone remotely controlled your computer and tried to hack into a government network. What a nightmare!

Actual content:

Imagine this nightmare scenario...

You check your e-mail program and it reports your username and password as no longer valid. You call your Internet service provider (ISP) to discuss the problem and they tell you they turned off your account due to "abuse". "Abuse!" you cry to the customer service operator, "What are you talking about?"

Example Outline Point(s): Tell the story of what happened when my friend got infected with a Trojan horse – make it dramatic. Tell people the consequences of having their ISP shut them down – make them feel the pain.

Actual content: "Someone used your computer this past Saturday night in an attempt to hack into a government computer system. They made the call at 1:20 a.m. from your phone number," replies the rep. "Look in your windows registry for a file called QAZWSX.hsq."

What you just read happened very recently to someone I know quite well. A computer hacker found an open port on his computer when he switched over from a dial-up Internet connection to an "always-on" high-speed connection.

Example Outline Point: Tell them exactly what dangers exist.

Actual content: The hacker used a robot scanning the Internet for available "ports", openings in a computer that allow data to pass back and forth from a network connection like the Internet. Once the hacker found an unprotected port on my friend's computer he simply inserted a Trojan Horse virus that rides along with Windows Notepad, a handy utility used by just about everyone who makes web pages.

When my friend activated the notepad program he also activated the virus. The virus in turn transmitted all of my friend's security information to the hacker and allowed him to gain access and control his victim's computer in the middle of the night.

Example Outline Point: Tell them why, how, and where to test their computer for vulnerability.

Actual content: Count me as the last person to sound paranoid, but, as always-on connections through DSL, cable, and T-1 lines proliferate, this story will repeat itself over and over until people learn to protect themselves from a very real threat.

Most people underestimate or rate completely ignorant about the importance of information they send over the Internet when surfing websites and checking email. Even if you only use a simple dial-up account, you can unknowingly transmit a significant amount of information, some of it quite personal.

You can analyze the security of your web connection for free by going to http://www.symantec.com/SecurityCheck/ . You can also verify the presence of any known viruses or Trojan horses on your computer. The information I saw when analyzing my personal computer frankly shocked me. I saw data I didn't even know about staring me right in the face after I performed this analysis.

Example Outline Point: Impress upon people how important your firewall and anti-virus software really are. Tell them how and where to find resources to prevent this from happening to them.

Actual content: To protect your computer hardware and sensitive data you should obtain a software package called a "firewall". A firewall, when combined with a good anti-virus program, helps stop unauthorized access on your computer, prevents virus infection, and "cloaks" your data ports against a hacker scanning for openings.

Symantec.com and McAfee.com both offer excellent personal firewall and anti-virus software from their websites or you can buy them off the shelf at your local office supply store.

Example conclusion idea from Section #6:

Go get yourself a good firewall and an anti-virus program. Everyone on the net needs these two tools and you should consider yourself totally irresponsible if you don't have them and keep them up to date.

Actual conclusion stated more simply:

A wise investment for anyone on the net... before it's too late!

Take the previous example at face value while you concentrate on fleshing out your outline and begin the first draft of your article.

Other than telling you to jumpstart your brain by pretending to write a letter to a friend, we would also offer this advice: **make your content succinct**.

By that we don't mean the same thing as keeping your article short or to ruthlessly edit at this point – far from it in fact! Most people can't spell succinct so think of concise or "to the point." Don't clutter your article with extra subject matter, which takes away from the thrust and central theme of the article.

If you want to write about the problems and solutions involved in setting up an autoresponder for your flower shop online, don't talk about overcoming chronic employee health problems – the two don't mix! Save that topic for another article. It will divert attention away from the thrust of your article and readers will wander elsewhere.

Also, you want to project a tone of sincerity in your prose. The easiest way to describe how to do this: get yourself really worked-up and enthusiastic about your subject and just write straight from your heart. Your enthusiasm and genuine care for your audience will carry the tone of sincerity into the fiber of your article and cause the text to just gush out of you – guaranteed!

EXERCISE FOR STEP #8 – WRITE YOUR ARTICLE BY FLESHING OUT YOUR OUTLINE

Here you put the rubber to the road and the pedal to the metal. Take your outline and write the first draft of your article. Try to make it come out between 600 to 1,000 words.

Caution: Don't fall back into the trap of the 5th grade where you had to write a 500 word essay on what you did last summer and you counted every word as you wrote (including a, the, but, & and!). To quickly gauge how many words you've written just use this rule of thumb:

Typing on your word processor in 12-point type, single space, Times New Roman font, with 1-inch borders all around the page, and a double space between paragraphs, a full typed page equals about 500 words.

So here you go. Look back at the outline you made so far and take one last look for any more attention-getting, high-impact points you can add before writing the first draft of your article.

Now write. Write! WRITE that article!

Step 9 – Edit Your Article Into a "Lean, Mean, Attention-Getting Machine"

After writing your article, the next job involves trimming or sculpting it into a finished product.

Well why would you want to edit something where you put in so much work? Why tear up something after you build it… that sounds crazy!

Welcome to the next phase of building a world-class article!

By the way, this same process applies whether editing your 500-word article or a 500,000 word novel or non-fiction work.

Now as we start wrapping up your article, let's take a look at it to see what you need to do to get it ready for your readers.

By the way, did you know that a movie director will shoot many hours of film and then turn it over to the film editors or producers to mold into a compact and tightly knit story? Most movies run in the hour and 45 minute range, but virtually all of them get trimmed down from 10 to 50 hours of initial shooting. That represents a 5:1 to 25:1 ratio of starting content to finished product.

Moral of the story – have no fear of trimming anything and everything that won't make your article a smashing success.

Go through the following four principles or approaches to editing and apply them to your rough article before proceeding to Section #10 on Polishing.

1. Understand the "Real" purpose of editing

A wood carver or sculptor starts with a large block of stone or wood and doesn't worry about the original bulk, because he or she knows that they will cut, trim and polish everything until they reveal the finished statue.

In other words, they remove everything that isn't the statue and leave only that which is the statue!

Do the same with your article to obtain the final result. Edit out anything that "isn't the article!"

It doesn't matter how much you put into the first draft because you wanted to get down all of the ideas, in much the same fashion that a builder first piles up the assorted material used in a house on the vacant lot. Consider your first draft as the total pile of building materials for your article.

Right now go through your article and look for points that don't seem to go anywhere or trail off into space without a concrete purpose. Either change or delete those points.

Next, look for areas where you repeat yourself. Often, when you "get on a roll" with a topic you feel great passion for, you'll say the same thing two or three times in a row. Eliminate the repetition unless you really need it for the sake of emphasis.

Finally, as you grow and develop your skills as an article writer, you'll find yourself naturally writing with the intention of trimming. This may sound at odds with our advice about writing generously, but not really. Follow the principles in planning the article and you'll find that your writing style will turn into a consistency where peeling away some of the text will not alter the meaning of the remaining parts of each paragraph.

Once you do it a few times you'll end up rattling off all the points you want to cover, putting them in order, expanding them by writing a few sentences about each point, and then go back during the editing process to slice out the parts that don't fit. This represents the true power of this 11 Step process we teach you.

2. Can you add anything?

Do you see anything now in your article where you could add something before getting to the polishing stage?

Very few of us can include everything the first time we take pen in hand or sit at the keyboard. Even making a list beforehand will not include every possibility because the creative process of actually writing the article will make you think of more things and additional points as you go along.

Only viewing the completed article will let you think of that extra little "tidbit" which might add something of great importance to your article.

During my insurance days I would make copious lists of topics I had to cover. After finishing these lists I would give them to a very smart lady who would look them over and then tell me the three or four things I forgot to include. So feel free to bring in your colleagues for a "back fence" review before proceeding, because it can help greatly. They can help you keep on the lookout for the missing piece you don't see.

Also, make sure to maintain a consistent style in the way you write your article. By doing so you can insert the after-thoughts into the text without doing a major rewrite!

3. Do you cover the topic completely?

Does your article give the reader a feeling of completion?

Don't leave the reader wondering about a major concern, which you skipped over too lightly. At the same time you want to leave a feeling that this article can follow up and connect with a topic of similar concern — in other words, make them see that this article represents just part of the "BIG" picture or the "tip of the iceberg."

"To Be Continued" — three words which often frustrated some of the older people who grew up at the movies on Saturday afternoons. The Saturday serial thriller which ended with the hero flying over the cliff in a

flaming car, made us want to come back next week to see how he got out of the scrape. But, though we came back, we sometimes felt tricked because the movie director showed a way out for him which we didn't see the previous week.

Avoid this problem with your articles.

Don't leave your readers hanging because you didn't finish the topic at hand. They want to know how to handle whatever issue you raise, so finish the job with no loose ends.

4. Stay away from the "wastebasket!"

Unless something makes absolutely no sense or sounds completely wrong, never throw away anything you deleted from the final article, especially big blocks of text.

Why?

Because you may just decide later that you can take the deleted portion and use it in another article! Often, what doesn't work in one place can work perfectly somewhere else.

Don't waste words and throw them away, you may need them somewhere else! We recycle articles and expand on them for other problems or subjects of major interest to people. Frankly, it might shock you if you realized the amount of recycling you could do, especially with a series of articles, and never get accused of running the same old material over and over.

Now don't take this to mean that you should endlessly repeat one or two articles over and over again. But, as time goes by, you will find yourself looking at old articles and putting new spins on them as circumstances change. One of the great things about the Internet — it always changes!

If you write an article about one certain aspect of an overall problem or subject that changes frequently you can always go back, update the article and distribute it again.

A final note on editing your article…

One obvious point you should not neglect in the editing stage — especially while thinking so hard on the four previous points — run a spelling and grammar check on your article!

Nothing leaves a bad taste in people's mouths like good writing with misspelled words in it. Yes, we rate as guilty as anyone else with the occasional spelling glitch and gaff, but you should take all the obvious steps to cut down on as many errors as possible.

EXERCISE FOR STEP #9 – EDITING YOUR ARTICLE

Take the four principles outlined under editing and apply them to your article before moving on to Section #10 on Polishing.

Use the following questions to make an effective editing pass at your article:

1. What (if anything) can you remove from the article so you make your points quickly, concisely and without detracting from your main purpose and subject?
2. What (if anything) can you add to the article to help the reader understand the subject even better?
3. Take a hard look at your article. Do you cover the topic completely and deliver on the expectations of the readers, or do you leave them feeling empty and without a feeling of completion?
4. Do you have any "left over" content you can use for a future or related article?
5. Did you do a spelling and grammar check?

Step 10 - Polishing Your Article

By now, the article you crafted as you went through each of the previous nine (9) sections should take shape nicely. Congratulations!

We took you around a lot of turns pretty fast and you may not have gotten everything 100% perfect, but you certainly got MUCH further than the vast majority of other people out there on the web! Pat yourself on the back right now!

Practice, practice and more of the same will let you get better. But hey, in the process of practicing you will drive hundreds and thousands of visitors to your site — what a deal!

EXERCISE FOR STEP #10 – POLISHING YOUR ARTICLE

Use the following checkpoints to get more "gloss" and to heighten the shine on your article:

1. Once you write the article and get ready for distribution you'll want to know "how it plays" as soon as possible. Go out and get criticism on the article from your business associates. Send the article and ask them to please look it over and tell you:

   a. Their overall opinion on the article: Excellent / Good / Poor

   b. How well it covers the subject: Excellent / Good / Poor

   c. Does it leave the reader with a feeling of: Completion / Emptiness / Desire to learn more

   d. Do they see any specific areas for improvement?

   e. What did they like most / least about the article?

2. Does your article have the potential to alienate any significant numbers of people or groups within your target audience? If so, can you tone down or modify that particular area without diluting your overall message or weakening your stand on the issue.

3. Put the article away for a day and "sleep on it!" Right now you feel too close to the article. You'll truly feel a sense of amazement at the areas you missed or the obvious areas for improvement once you put the article away for a day or two and come back to it with a fresh set of eyes.

4. 24-48 hours later when you come back to your article, ask yourself:

   a. Do I see any areas where I can obviously improve my writing or my message?

   b. Do I see anything that might alienate the ezine editors or website owners where I want to publish or post my articles? If so, fix it.

c. Does the article fit the persona or "voice" I said I wanted to portray in Step #7? If not, how can I modify it to fit that voice, or do I even need to? Maybe the natural voice that came out works better than the voice you thought you wanted to convey.

All of us carry a built in sensitivity or "pride of authorship" and we will see things differently from the way others see them.

Whether you have just written your first article or your 200th article, it always helps to ask a group of your acquaintances to read and comment on your article and pay attention to their helpful comments. This will help you spot trends — both good and bad.

If 10 out of 12 people come up with the same criticism then it might carry some validity and you can make adjustments accordingly. If another 9 or 10 out of 12 come up with praise for your approach — then you just might have a winner.

Side NOTE: Often the feedback you get from your associates as well as people who read your article on your website and in ezines will help you get ideas for new articles! Pay attention, especially to the questions they ask, as those questions very often contain the seeds for even better and more penetrating articles.

Finally, see if you can find some articles written by others on the same or similar subjects to yours. Compare your article to others with the same eye as if you belonged to your target audience. Look for any glaring points you left out or look for additional resources you could easily include and massively increase the value of your article without much work.

Ad agencies always scout out the competition when ads appear on TV, radio, newspapers and magazines. Grocery stores check out each other's ads in the Sunday papers to see how their pricing compares. Gas stations constantly monitor each other for that slight pricing advantage during different times of the workweek and weekend. So you must also look at your competitors' articles and honestly grade them compared to your own efforts.

Would you feel inclined to click on their resource box? If so, then they must own something pretty good you can model for this or future articles!

Step 11 - Three critical parts of any highly effective article.

Take one last step back from your article to make sure it contains these 3 key elements:

1) An attention getting headline that speaks directly to the minds of your target audience, such as "War Declared on Spammers".

   Whatever you do, don't release your article until you feel like you have a headline that will grab members of your target audience by the brain and suck them in so they'll feel like complete idiots if they don't stop their current activity and read your article.

   Does your article's headline do this?

   If necessary, spend an hour or two brainstorming better headlines for your article. Look at other successful headlines and model them.

2) Make sure the body of your article clearly and completely covers the topic as promised in the headline.

   Don't leave anyone with a feeling of emptiness, nor do you want to "give away the store." Experiment to find that perfect balance where readers get what they expected from your article and it leads them very naturally to want even more of what you offer. Doing this will get them to move on to step three...

3) The conclusion of your article should very naturally lead the reader to the call to action—especially so they'll click on your resource

box and visit your website, sign up for your mini-course, or send you an email.

Here's the spot where you "cash in" on all your hard work. Don't drop the ball here just as you get ready to go over the goal line!

Special Section: Put A Better "High-Gloss Finish" On Your Article Than Most "Professional" Writers!

— OR—

"TEN Words You Should Try Never To Use When Writing Articles!"

In this section we'll show you a technique to make your writing stand out head and shoulders above even those "professional" writers who "write for a living!" Not one in 100 writers knows about, let alone applies, this final technique to their writing. Those who do create articles, essays and books which far outshine their competition.

Though you obviously can't retrain yourself in one day, you *can* start to incorporate this technique into your article writing style to make quantum leaps in the overall quality and "polish" of your writing.

We want to eliminate (or dramatically reduce the use of) ten words from writing in general; we call them the ten "crutch" words which guarantee the destruction of good, smooth writing on any topic.

If you look back over the past sixty or so pages you will see that we rarely used the ten "crutch" words except where it seemed completely unavoidable to do so.

What ten words could cause such damage in writing? Namely:

- am
- are
- is
- was
- were
- be
- been
- have
- has
- had

There, we did it! We took a stand which will bring down the wrath of literary folks everywhere who love these ten words. Without them they couldn't turn out endless pages of drivel and stilted prose, which sometimes equals the Valley-speak and the "Like you know" users today.

Think about all the articles and ebooks you read and start looking for these words scattered throughout the pages. We sometimes count four or five "is" and "was" usages in a single sentence. You might not understand the sentence without rereading it a couple of times. We especially like the use of "had had" in a sentence – not!

The English language provides a broad field on which to play and paint word pictures, but we spend most of our time down one back alley behind a dumpster because of those ten words.

Do we use those ten words when we talk, of course! But turn them off, throw them away, and try to write without them and you'll amaze yourself at how you'll make everything sound low-key, informal and directed personally at your readers.

We rode the "was and is" trail as much as anyone else in school and in the work-a-day world. One time Dallas submitted a manuscript to a literary agent, who also taught creative writing at a very prestigious university. She liked the content and told him to change the style of using all of the "to be" verbs" which bugged her no end from all the manuscripts she received. Dallas took one look and said, "Right!"

For some reason this clicked automatically and he never looked back after that in all of his writing. He them imparted that style to his son, Jim, who tries diligently to follow his father's example.

It will amaze you how the smoothness of this "direct voice" almost lulls people into acceptance of what you write because they can scan through it much easier from not tripping over the crutch connector words which slow the flow.

Successful articles produce results because they flow in such a way that readers' minds don't need to work to understand what you want to tell them. This approach works better than anything we've found so far, so take a look at the examples below and see if they don't trigger some ideas within you for making your writing flow much more smoothly.

Before:

> The dog is black. The dog is big. The dog is my friend. He is a long-haired dog. He is my guard and looks for me after school. He was two years old when we got him. He is a Labrador retriever.

Does this style of composition sound familiar? Unfortunately most of us never get beyond this way of writing. We just add in more words. Now take a look at the revision and see if you find it somewhat more interesting, informative and just plain more pleasant to read!

> Meet Jake, my best friend and protector. This long-haired, black, two hundred pound Labrador Retriever looks for me every day after school. We got him just after his second birthday three years ago.

Now, which sounds more interesting and informative? Which flows better?

Of course you can't automatically switch over and write in this style, we understand that. It takes practice. Look back over the past sixty pages and study the prose and lack of those ten words.

We went through quite a training session to eliminate most of the passive words and start using "action words". For every sentence using those

ten "no-no" words you can find an alternative direct voice or active verb which will improve the understanding and content of your article.

A few more examples on how to restate sentences to give power and impact for your readers:

1. It is time to pet the cat = I want to pet the cat now.
2. The car has squeaky springs and is uncomfortable = My 1974 car's squeaky springs ride very uncomfortably on bumpy roads.
3. The computer desk is hard for me to use. = My posture, along with the keyboard height, makes it hard to operate the computer.
4. It is hard to keep up with my email and to get it done each day. = Responding to an average of 50 customer service emails takes up most of my workday.
5. This is the best software I've ever seen for solving the virus problem we have been dealing with. = In my opinion, this software rates the best for fighting the virus epidemic we all face at this time.

Anytime you use the ten words in a sentence, think how you can strengthen the statement while also inserting additional, relevant information.

As a final step, if you'll accept the challenge, go back through your article and look for these words:

- am
- are
- is
- was
- were
- be
- been
- have
- has
- had

When you spot them do your level best to rewrite the sentence until it reads in a much more direct and active voice. Don't stop until you eliminate at least half the total instances of the ten "crutch" words in your article. Then read the two versions of your article and decide for yourself which sounds better.

Congratulations! If you followed all 11 steps laid out so far in the book, along with this special section, you now own a pretty darn good article! You should feel really good right now and very proud of yourself!

The next section provides a valuable article "Blueprint" you can use for producing all your articles in the future. Take a look through that section and then let's move on to Part 2 of "Turn Words Into Traffic," using the article you just wrote to drive traffic to your website!

Your Money-Making Article "Blueprint"

This article blueprint will help you in quickly crafting all future articles. You may even want to print it off and keep it in a place you can find easily. It summarizes all the assignments covered in the first half of "Turn Words Into Traffic" and will prove quite valuable as you create and distribute future articles.

1. Targeting

In one sentence, write out whom you want to target with your article:

____

____

____

2. Brainstorming

Fill in each blank as best you can. As you go through each one you'll start to see a pattern or a high level of interest on your part in a particular area. In other words – the lights will go on and you'll "know" the topic of the article you want to write.

- I want to help people with their problems in the following areas?
- What breaking news or current events affect my target audience right now?
- What recent industry, general, or technology changes can or will affect your target audience in the foreseeable future?

- The five most frequently asked questions you see from people in your target audience? These would include questions either emailed to you or posted in forums & discussion groups.
- Look at two recent articles by others which you can use as a springboard for your articles. How could you take a different view on the same issues in each article? How can you expand on what they've already written? How can you take the same topic in both articles and put your own spin on the critical areas of each article?
- **Now choose your topic** for your article and write it clearly here as a statement of your intention!

___

___

___

3. Choose Your Outcome

State exactly what action you want people to take as a result of reading your article.

Example:

As a result of reading my article I want members of my target audience to get excited enough to click the link to my website to get more information about my ebook because it solves a specific problem they have.

Write down the outcome you want from your article now:

___

___

___

___

___

4. Make Your Article Subject Irresistible

If you still haven't written down a headline that summarizes a very attractive reason to read your article, let's go through these steps.

1. Write three statements or headlines which promise strong benefits to the reader.
2. Write three statements, which will arouse curiosity for potential readers who belong to your target audience.
3. Write three statements you could write an article about which would scare the "Bejabbers" off people if they knew of them.
4. Based on what you've written above, create or choose the absolutely most irresistible headline right now.

5. Outline the Points You Want to Cover

1. **Write down the main topic or concern which will serve as the subject of your article:**

 ____

 ____

2. **Write down the five main points which make up the thrust of your article**

 1. ______________________________
 2. ______________________________
 3. ______________________________
 4. ______________________________
 5. ______________________________

3. **Write down any quotes or references which apply to your article:**

 ____

 ____

 ____

 ____

4. **Write down any and all additional points which you should include in the article** (don't worry about putting them in the correct order at this point).

____

____

5. **Write down the conclusion your article should lead people to after reading it.** This can represent an action you want them to take (secure their computer against hackers), an opinion you want them to adopt (all hackers are scum), or even just to acknowledge the topic in the first place ("Wow, I didn't realize how vulnerable my computer actually is! I need to take action.")

____

____

6. Organize Your Points Into A Structure

1. **Write out the introductory thought you want to introduce with your article.**

   ____

   ____

   Example: Imagine trying to access your email only to discover your Internet access had been cancelled because someone remotely controlled your computer and tried to hack into a government computer. What a nightmare!

2. **Arrange the points of your article in the step-by-step order you will cover them.**

   1. ____
   2. ____
   3. ____
   4. ____
   5. ____

3. **Write out the concluding thought you want people to draw from your article when they finish reading.**

____

____

____

7. Choose Your Voice Or Writing Style

Write out a brief statement of the voice you'll use to deliver your articles and make your individual mark on the minds of your readers.

____

____

____

Example:

I want my writing style to project the image of an approachable, yet extremely knowledgeable person who provides valuable information in a way that members of my target audience can use and benefit from immediately.

8. Write Your Article By Fleshing Out Your Outline

Take your outline and write the first draft of your article. Try to make it come out between 600 to 1,000 words.

Caution: Don't fall back into the trap of the 5th grade where you had to write a 500-word essay on what you did last summer and you counted every word as you wrote.

To quickly gauge how many words you've written just use this rule of thumb: Typing on your word processor in 12-point type, single space, Times New Roman font, with 1-inch borders all around the page, a full typed page equals about 500 words.

Now WRITE!

9. Edit Your Article

Use the following questions to make an effective editing pass at your article:

1. What (if anything) can you remove from the article so you make your points quickly, concisely and without detracting from your main purpose and subject?

2. What (if anything) can you add to the article to help the reader understand the subject even better?

3. Take a hard look at your article. Do you cover the topic completely and deliver on the expectations of the readers or do you leave them feeling empty and without a feeling of completion?

4. Do you have any "leftover" content you can use for a future or related article?

5. Did you do a spelling and grammar check?

10. Polishing Your Article

Use the following checkpoints to get more "shoe polish" to heighten the shine on your article:

1. Go out and get criticism on the article from your business associates. Send the article and ask them to please look it over and tell you:
    1. Their overall opinion on the article: Excellent / Good / Poor
    2. How well it covers the subject: Excellent / Good / Poor
    3. Does it leave the reader with a feeling of: Completion / Emptiness / Desire to learn more
    4. Do they see any specific areas for improvement?
    5. What did they like most / least about the article?

2. Does your article have the potential to alienate any significant numbers of people or groups within your target audience? If so, can you tone down or modify that particular area without diluting your overall message or weakening your stand on the issue.

3. Put the article away for a day and "sleep on it!" Come back to it with a fresh set of eyes tomorrow and give it a through going over.

4. When you come back to your article 24 hours later, ask yourself:
    1. Do I see any areas where I can obviously improve my writing or my message?
    2. Do I see anything that might alienate the ezine editors or website owners I want to publish or post my articles? If so, fix it.
    3. Does the article fit the persona or "voice" I said I wanted to portray in Step #7? If not, how can I modify it to fit that voice – or do I even need to?

11. Three Key Parts of Any Highly Successful Article

Take one last step back from your article to make sure it contains these 3 key elements:

1. An attention getting headline that speaks directly to the minds of your target audience, such as "War Declared on Spammers".

   Does your article's headline do this?

2. Make sure the body of your article clearly and completely covers the topic as promised in the headline. Don't leave anyone with a feeling of emptiness, nor do you want to "give away the store."

3. The conclusion leads the reader to the call to action— especially so they'll click on your resource box and visit your website, sign up for your mini-course or send you an email. Here's the spot where you "cash in" on all your hard work.

12. Put Your Article Into The "Active" Voice

See how many of the 10 "crutch" words you can eliminate from your article to make it read more smoothly and effectively for your readers. Try to eliminate at least half the instances you use them and then judge for yourself whether or not your article reads better.

- am
- be
- are
- been

- is
- was
- were
- have
- has
- had

PART 2

Specific Techniques for Promoting With Your Articles

In this second section we'll teach you from A-Z how to find, approach, persuade and motivate ezine editors and website owners to run your articles. We'll also show you how to convert your article into a 24/7 profit generator!

Getting Your Article Physically Ready for Distribution

Formatting Your Article Text

You'll greatly improve your chances of success if you send your article pre-formatted to Ezine editors, publishers or web site owners so they can immediately use it by simply by copying and pasting from the text you send them.

Typically, these people want a 60-character width, plain text, with hard carriage returns at the end of each line. Also, you'll improve your chances if you compile the statistics about your article and post these at the very top of the article.

Here is a sample of a pre-formatted article ready to send. Take a look at the article as a whole and then we'll discuss each part of the article individually.

Then we'll show you how to physically format the article using my (Jim's) favorite text editor "**Note Tab Lite**".

word count: 514
character width: 60
resource box: 4 lines + web link to “eBook Secrets Exposed”

==================================

3 Secrets to “Striking it Rich” in Cyberspace

- by Jim Edwards

http://www.thenetreporter.com

==================================

In the few seconds it takes you to read this another domain name gets registered at www.NetworkSolutions.com, the Internet’s oldest and largest domain name registrar.

Despite the “dot-bomb” era we just experienced, it seems everyone from industrial giants to corner flower shops still wants to stake a profitable claim in cyberspace.

The lure of low startup costs compared to brick-and-mortar operations and the promise of high rewards draws an ever-increasing crowd of merchants to the online marketplace.

Yet despite the optimism statistics tell us that 80% of these “e” businesses will fail within their first 12 months of operation.

People from all over the world ask me what it takes to succeed in the e-commerce world once they complete the basic steps for getting online.

The following three keys virtually *guarantee success* for any online enterprise.

The First Key:

A Quality product or service with highly evident and readily understood benefits for consumers.

If your product or service does not represent the highest quality and value possible, and if consumers don't understand exactly why they should buy from you, the speed of the Internet will just expose your shortcomings to the marketplace that much quicker.

In the offline world a product's benefits, not the features, cause consumers to make buying decisions.

A man doesn't buy a car with a 5 liter engine because of the horsepower, he buys it for the feeling of supremacy and control he thinks it will give him.

Kids don't want a 2.4gHz computer for computing power in doing homework, they want to play the latest games.

The Internet magnifies this "what's in it for me" benefits- driven evaluation by consumers.

Products or services presented with readily understood, self-serving benefits for consumers sell best online (and off).

The Second Key:

An excellent website that loads fast, provides pertinent information to targeted consumers, and allows them to make online purchases quickly and securely.

Your website should:

- Load fast by making conservative use of graphics. (Go to yahoo.com for an excellent example.)
- Provide exactly the information your potential customers want and need to make a purchase decision.
- Make it extremely easy for surfers to navigate your site and find exactly what they want.

- Look good on both the Netscape and Internet Explorer web-browsers at various screen resolutions and color settings. (640x480, 800x600, etc.).

The Third Key:

Consistent, targeted website traffic by consumers capable of buying your product or service.

Imagine buying a 50 foot billboard and, instead of putting it out by the highway, you hid it in your basement.

Nobody would see it!

The same thing happens if you don't actively and continuously promote your website to attract visitors.

With its incredible speed and communications power, the Internet acts as a magnifying glass for any organization's strengths and weaknesses. E-commerce, email, and a website won't do the job of marketing, selling, and customer service for any company.

They will, however, help every organization perform all of those business functions better, faster, and less expensively with the real and tangible result of "striking it rich" in cyberspace!

==================================

Jim Edwards is co-author of the NEW "eBook Secrets Exposed": How to making MASSIVE Amounts of Money - In Record Time - With Your Own eBook!

WHY are some people getting positively RICH selling ebooks?

Click Here Now ==> http://www.ebooksecretsexposed.com

** Attn Ezine editors / Site owners **

Feel free to reprint this article in its entirety in your ezine or on your site so long as you leave all links in place, do not modify the content and include our resource box as listed above.

If you need additional articles, check out my article archive for fresh, new content you can use on your website or in your ezine - FREE! http://www.infomarketingupdate.com/archive/

If you do use the material please send us a note so we can take a look. Thanks.

Feel free to substitute your affiliate link in place of our link in the resource box.

Earn 50% on every purchaser you refer.

Affiliate details are available here: http://www.ebookfire.com

Typically, your formatted ezine articles will follow this, or a similar format.

Section 1 – Article Stats

At the top of the article, you'll tell the total words in the article, as well as the line width of the article in characters, again typically 60 characters wide. This lets a prospective ezine editor know exactly how the article is formatted and how many words it contains. (I'll show you how to quickly and easily get that word count in the next section.)

Some ezine editors won't accept articles over or under a certain length… that's why I always try to keep mine right around 500-600 words. That length seems to fit the largest number of editors' preferences.

If I'm trying to get other people to promote the article to their lists as my affiliate, I will also include information about the resources box at the end of the article as well as which of my products I am promoting in that resource box. If I'm just trying to get them to run my article then I leave out that information.

word count: 490

character width: 60

resource box: 4 lines + web link to "eBook Secrets Exposed"

Section 2 – Title Section

Next, put the title at the top along with your name and copyright notice. You can even try putting your website address in there too (Caution: only attempt this if it's appropriate – trust your gut instinct as to whether or not to try it). Having your straight web address published like this will help increase clickthroughs to your website as well as help your search engine popularity when website owners post your article on their websites.

Also, putting your copyright information at the top this way will also help build your name recognition and your status as an expert.

==================================

3 Secrets to "Striking it Rich" in Cyberspace

- by Jim Edwards

(c) Jim Edwards - All Rights reserved

http://www.thenetreporter.com

==================================

Section 3 – The Body of the Article

Next, insert the body of the article itself between the bottom of the title box and the top of the resource box.

===================================

article text in between the top and bottom bar

TEXT TEXT

TEXT TEXT

===================================

Jim Edwards & David Garfinkel are co-authors of the NEW "eBook Secrets Exposed": How to make MASSIVE Amounts of Money - In Record Time - With Your Own eBook!

WHY are some people getting positively RICH selling ebooks? Click Here Now ==> http://www.ebooksecretsexposed.com

Section 4 – Your Resource Box

===================================

Jim Edwards & David Garfinkel are co-authors of the NEW "eBook Secrets Exposed": How to make MASSIVE Amounts of Money - In Record Time - With Your Own eBook!

WHY are some people getting positively RICH selling ebooks?

Click Here Now => http://www.turnwordsintotraffic.com/ese.html

Directly under the article you want to insert your resource box. This resource box helps you convince people to take whatever action you want as a result of reading your article. Most typically that action means either having them click over to your website or sign up for your free mini-course.

Section 5 – The "Pass-Along" Reprint Instructions Box

** Attn Ezine editors / Site owners **

Feel free to reprint this article in its entirety in your ezine or on your site so long as you leave all links in place, do not modify the content and include our resource box as listed above.

If you need additional articles, check out my article archive for fresh, new content you can use on your website or in your ezine - FREE!

http://www.infomarketingupdate.com/archive/

Underneath all of this you can include any reprint instructions for people who may read the article and want to pass it along or publish it in their own ezine or on their website. If you set up your own article announcement service (and I highly recommend you do) then you can also direct them to the sign-up sheet or website that gets them on your list for regular emails of your new articles.

Section 6 – The Affiliate Recruiting Clause

Feel free to substitute your affiliate link in place of our link in the resource box.

Earn 50% on every purchaser you refer.

Affiliate details are available here: http://www.ebookfire.com

FACT: Nothing motivates some people to run your article like cold, hard cash!

You can recruit a whole lot of affiliates really quickly if you publish articles that promote a specific product in your resource box and then encourage people to signup and put their affiliate link in your resource box before they publish it.

Do I do this with all my articles? No, but when I send out articles to my announcement list or to my affiliates I do because it massively increases the distribution since people can make money by publishing my content.

Please note: Each individual ezine editor and announcement website you pursue to share your article with their list, may have their own rules. However, if you format your article the way we've just covered, you will basically have everything right at your fingertips and can easily modify your information to meet any individual's specific requirements.

Now, let's talk about additional information you should have available before submitting your articles…

Additional Information you should have available when submitting articles:

Many article announcement sites, as well as some ezines, will require you to provide additional information while submitting articles, including:

- article descriptions of various lengths
- relevant keywords
- information about the author (in this case, you).

Not all of them require exactly the same data, but many do.

To speed the process of submitting your articles, I have found that having the following information available in "**Note Tab Lite**" ready to copy and paste into various web forms will greatly speed up the submission process.

- ❑ Title
- ❑ Author Name
- ❑ Author email
- ❑ url (web address) leading to the article on your website
- ❑ automatic autoresponder for the article
- ❑ word count on the article
- ❑ 5-20 keywords separated by commas describing the article
- ❑ 20-30 word description of the article
- ❑ Brief 3 to 4 sentence author bio

- ❑ 3 line, 5 line AND 6 line resource box
- ❑ Reprint guidelines
- ❑ The article itself with only the title and author name, copyright at the top
- ❑ Have available an 80x105 pixel photograph in .jpg format to send along to anyone who requests it.

Here's an example of the information I prepared ahead of time for another article I sent out with great response and positive sales results. I simply have it all ready in "**Note Tab Lite**" to copy and paste so when I start submitting, it goes bam-bam-bam… one right after another.

Title: Cheap Web Hosting is NO Bargain!

Author: Jim Edwards

author email: jim@thenetreporter.com

url: http://www.thenetreporter.com/cheap-web-hosting.shtml

autoresponder: mailto:cheaphost@33daystoonlineprofits.com

word count: 500

keywords:

cheap web hosting, bargain web host, host my site, ftp, domain name

20-30 word description:

$4.95 web hosting may sound like a great deal... but you won't think so when your business gets shut down without WARNING!

Author Bio:

Jim Edwards, a.k.a. TheNetReporter.com, is a nationally known speaker, author, syndicated newspaper columnist and web developer. Owner of several successful e-businesses as well as a professional e-business consulting firm, Jim's writing comes straight off the front lines of the Internet and e-commerce.

3 Line Resource Box

-=-

You can start with a few bucks and a good idea to make lots of money online! I did, and I'll teach you how no matter what product you sell=> http://www.33daystoonlineprofits.com

-=-

5 Line Resource Box

-=-

How much would you pay to get day-by-day instructions from 2 top Internet marketing experts every day for 33 days? You can start with a few bucks and a good idea to make lots of money online! I did, and I'll teach you how no matter what product you sell! ==> http://www.33daystoonlineprofits.com

-=-

6 Line Resource Box

-=-

How much would you pay to get day-by-day instructions from 2 top Internet marketing experts every day for 33 days?

** How about 88 cents? **

You can start with a few bucks and a good idea to make lots of money online! I did, and I'll teach you how no matter what product you sell! ==> http://www.33daystoonlineprofits.com

-=-

Reprint Guidelines:

** Attn Ezine editors / Site owners **

Feel free to reprint this article in its entirety in your ezine or on your site so long as you leave all links in place, do not modify the content and include our resource box as listed above.

Now let's take a look at my favorite tool for quickly formatting text and having it ready to copy and paste at a moment's notice...

Note Tab Light - A quick, easy, and FREE formatting tool:

My favorite tool for quickly formatting my article text to the proper character width and compiling the text statistics is "**Note Tab Lite**,"available free at www.notetab.com. Please note, we make no commission by advising you to get this program... so our recommendation is extremely genuine!

Here's how you use Note Tab Lite to format your article in just a few simple steps.

Once you have written your article in your word processor, checked for spelling and punctuation errors and reviewed it, you're ready to format. You want to format your article in plain ASCII text because it makes it much easier to paste the text into web-based submission forms as well as into emails to ezine publishers.

After you have downloaded and installed Note Tab Lite, follow these instructions to quickly format your text.

1. First, set up Note Tab Lite to wrap your text width to 60 characters. You do this because that's the character width most ezine editors want text formatted to ensure a consistent look when emailing.

2. Click "View" on the menu bar at the top and then click "Options"

3. This brings up the "**Options**" screen where you want to click the "**Documents**" tab in order to set the width of the text.

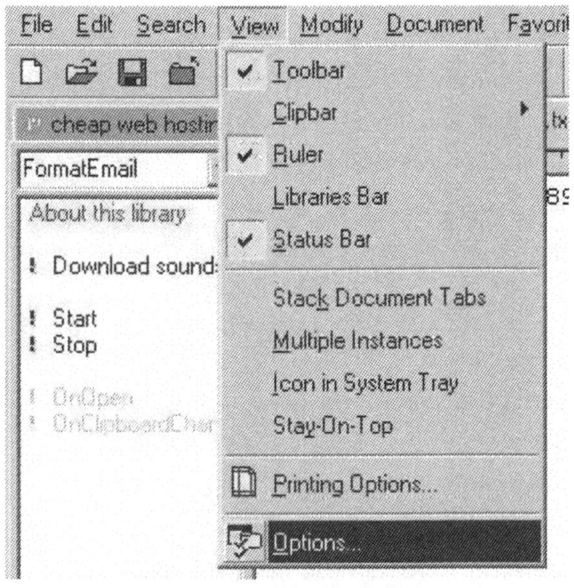

4. After clicking the "**Documents**" tab, make sure to check the box next to "**Word Wrap**" and also next to "**Wrap to Column**." Then fill in the box next to "Wrap to Column" with the number **60**. This will cause your text to wrap at 60 characters wide – the standard width for most email publishers.

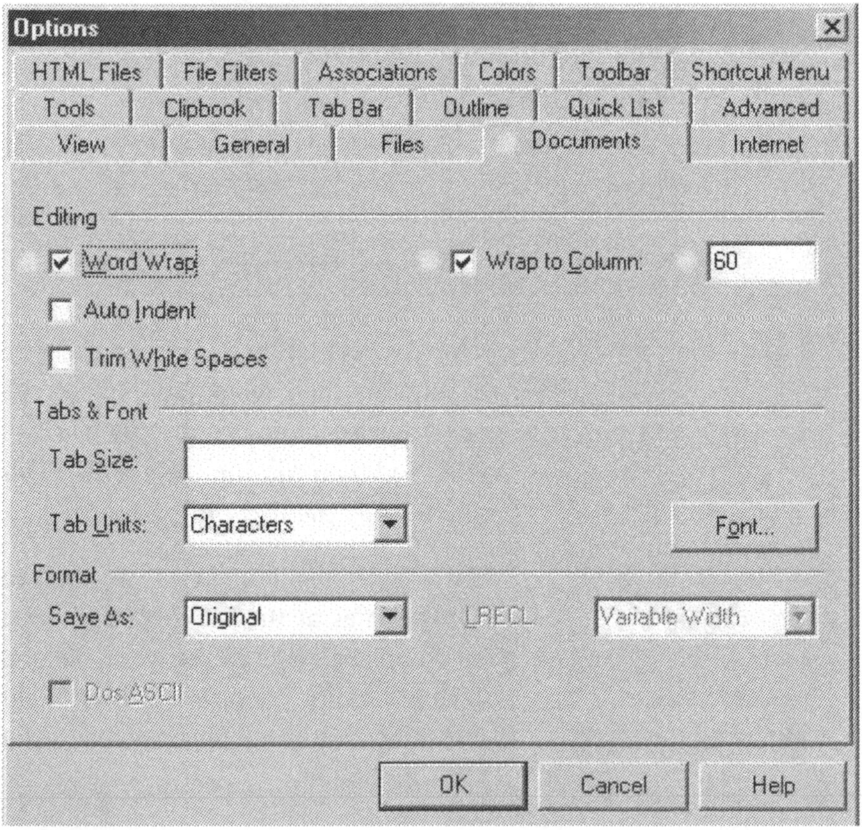

5. Then click the "OK" button.

6. Next, click the blank page icon in the upper left hand corner of the screen to open a new, blank document. Copy and paste the text of your article from your word processor into the Note Tab Light screen.

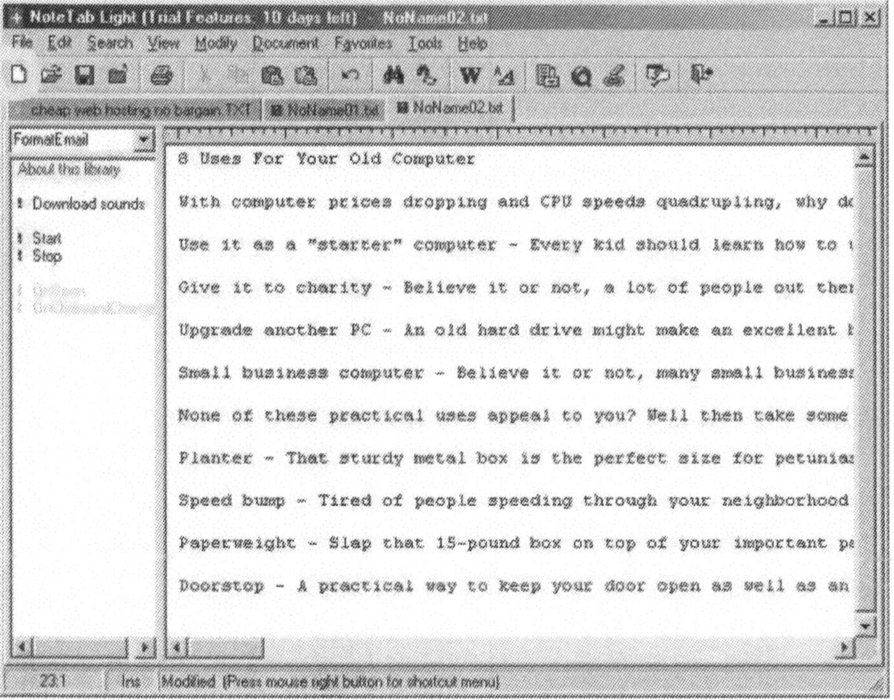

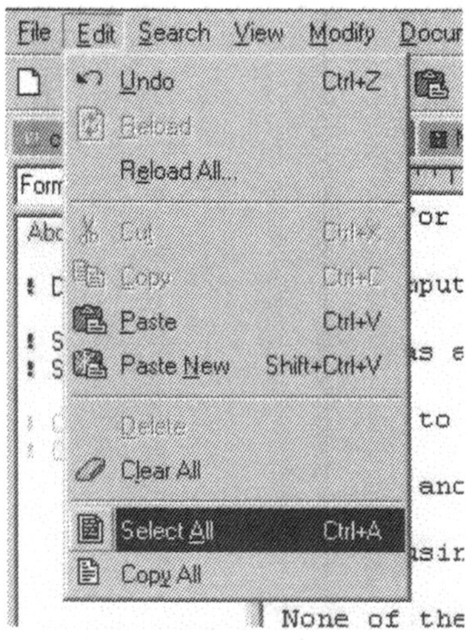

7. Next, select all the text of your article so you can then wrap the text at the proper width. You do this by clicking "**Edit**" and then clicking "**Select All.**" This will select all the text on the page.

8. After selecting all the text you want to split the lines at the 60 character mark. You do this by going to the menu bar and clicking "Modify" then "Lines" then "Split Lines." This will cause the lines to wrap at the proper point.

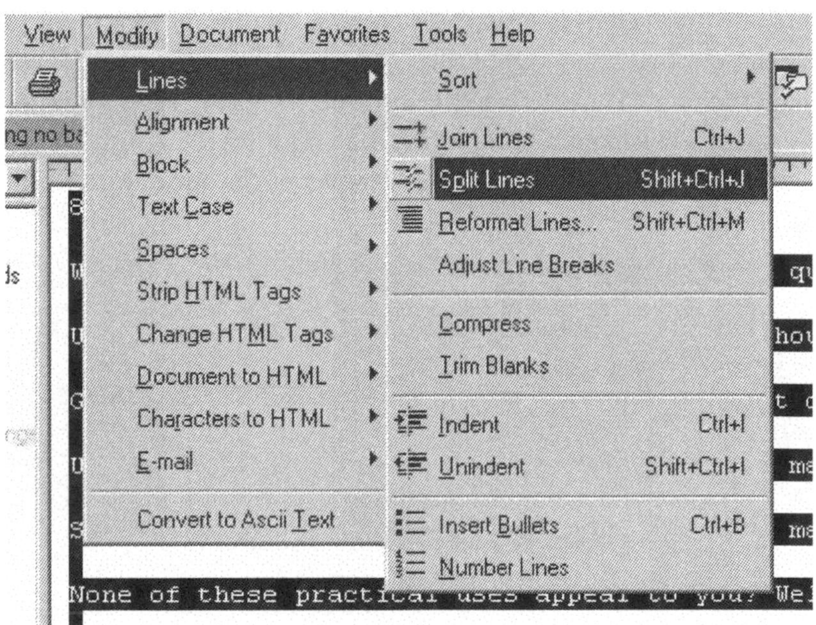
View
Modify
Document
Favorites
Tools
Help
Lines
Alignment
Block
Text Case
Spaces
Strip HTML Tags
Change HTML Tags
Document to HTML
Characters to HTML
E-mail
Convert to Ascii Text
Sort
Join Lines Ctrl+J
Split Lines Shift+Ctrl+J
Reformat Lines... Shift+Ctrl+M
Adjust Line Breaks
Compress
Trim Blanks
Indent Ctrl+I
Unindent Shift+Ctrl+I
Insert Bullets Ctrl+B
Number Lines

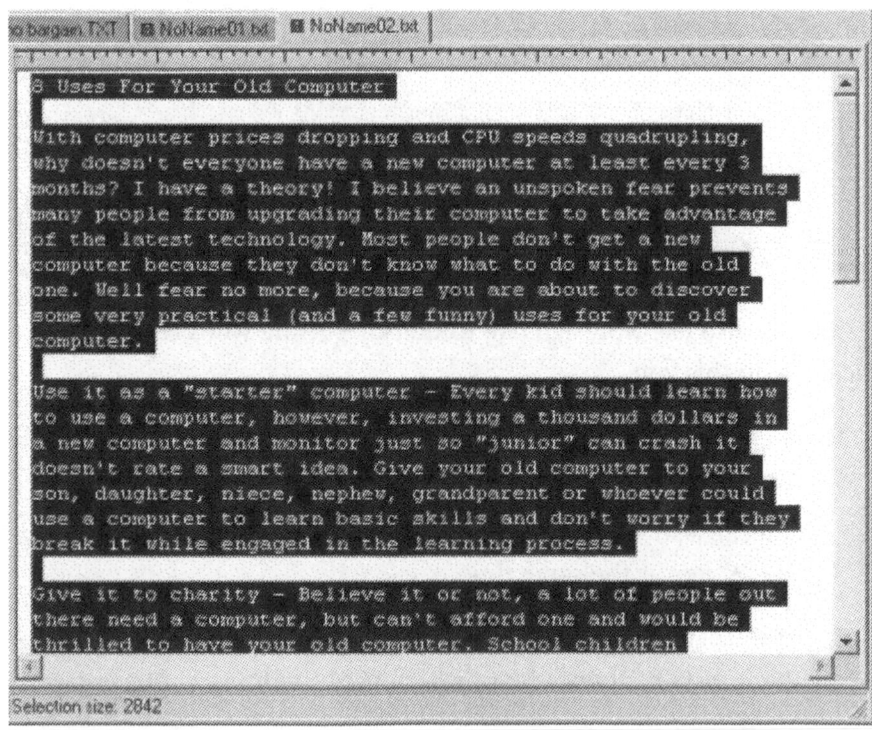
NoName01.txt
NoName02.txt
8 Uses For Your Old Computer
With computer prices dropping and CPU speeds quadrupling, why doesn't everyone have a new computer at least every 3 months? I have a theory! I believe an unspoken fear prevents many people from upgrading their computer to take advantage of the latest technology. Most people don't get a new computer because they don't know what to do with the old one. Well fear no more, because you are about to discover some very practical (and a few funny) uses for your old computer.
Use it as a "starter" computer - Every kid should learn how to use a computer, however, investing a thousand dollars in a new computer and monitor just so "junior" can crash it doesn't rate a smart idea. Give your old computer to your son, daughter, niece, nephew, grandparent or whoever could use a computer to learn basic skills and don't worry if they break it while engaged in the learning process.
Give it to charity - Believe it or not, a lot of people out there need a computer, but can't afford one and would be thrilled to have your old computer. School children
Selection size: 2842

9. I know this seems like skipping ahead a tiny bit, but I wanted to point out that now I would then paste in or type in the rest of the information I know I'll need to provide, as I start submitting my articles. I have found that putting it all right there in Note Tab (so I can easily copy and paste) greatly improves the speed with which I am able to submit my article(s).

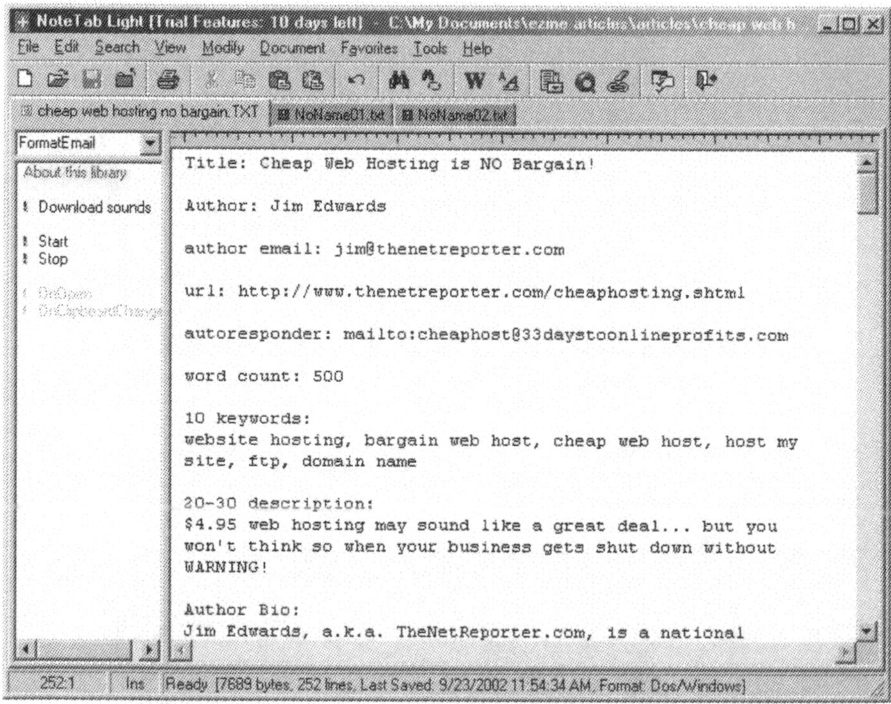

You can also use Note Tab Lite to quickly get the word count for your article. To do this you:

1. Highlight all the text of your article. Do this by following the instructions in #7 above.

   You can also select all the text by holding down the "Ctrl" key plus the "A" key at the same time.

2. After highlighting all the text in your article, on the Menu Bar at the top click "**Tools**" then click "**Text Statistics**".

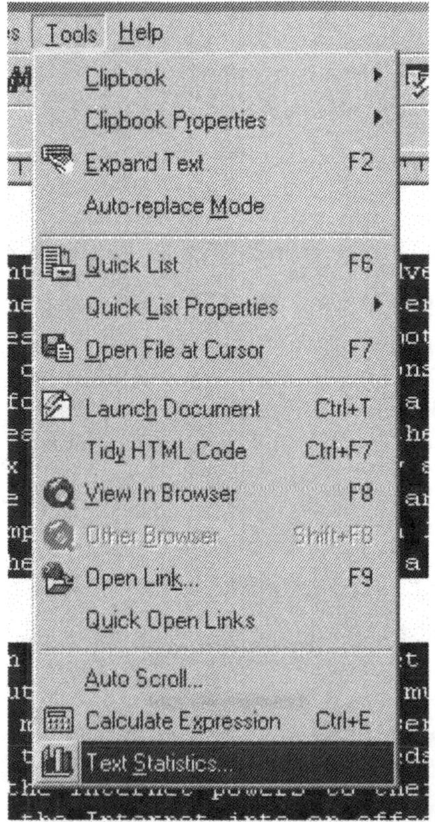

3. The program will then display a box telling you how many words make up your article.

So there you have it – a step-by-step guide for using one of the best free tools I have ever found for quickly formatting your article text and getting it ready to send off to ezine editors and announcement sites. The more you use it, the more you'll like it. I would also encourage you to investigate all the other features of Note Tab. If you do anything with HTML or web pages, this editor makes searching and replacing text in multiple documents an absolute breeze.

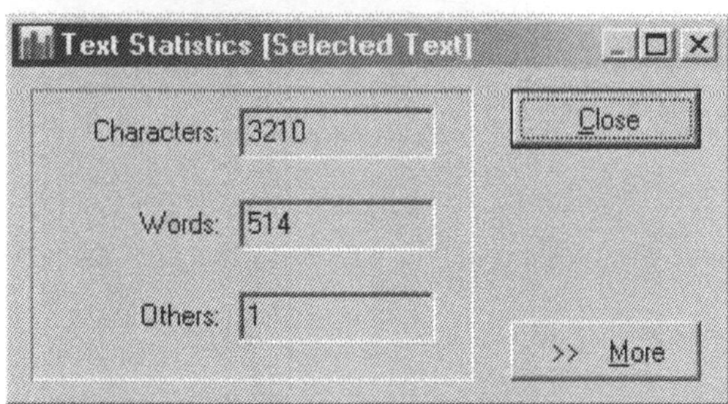

You're almost ready to start submitting your article, but there's one last thing you need to turn your article into a traffic — and profit — generating machine…

Creating a Compelling Resource Box

Your article's content will prove you have the expertise or targeted information your readers want, but now you need to get people to act on it in a way that drives website traffic, creates customers and builds your business.

You do this with your "resource box" – a small amount of formatted text, usually placed at the end of an article, that gives readers information about how to find out more about you, your products, or your services.

A compelling resource box at the end of your article rates just as important as the article itself because here you take them from just a "reader" and turn them into a "customer" or a "subscriber".

The resource box acts as the cash register which enables you to get "paid" for providing the article content... and the quality of your resource box determines how well you do at taking readers and getting them into your sales cycle.

In reality, people can only take one of three actions when it comes to your resource box:

1. click a website link;
2. send an email to an autoresponder to request a free report or enroll in a mini-course;
3. send *you* an email.

But they can only do these things once they read your article and see your resource box!

An Effective Resource Box

Let me state very clearly that almost ***every*** resource box that gets people to take action contains each and every one of these parts:

1. First, it has a headline or opening sentence that really <u>snatches</u> **attention.**

Similar in many ways to a classified ad, a resource box grabs readers, usually with the promise of a huge benefit they will receive or serious problem they will avoid by taking action NOW.

2. Second, you use the body of your resource box to build interest once you get their attention.

   You do this by providing a small nugget of very tantalizing information that builds on the promise made in the headline. Often a result or tangible evidence supporting the promise works well. (We'll give you some examples in just a few pages from now.)

3. Third, you use a "closer," where you drive people to action, usually with something as simple as "click here to get a free email," "click here to get a free mini-course," "click here to get a free report," "click here to get more information," and then a link either to a website or an email address.

   Space allowing, you can insert a little bullet such as => in front of the link to help people automatically know exactly what to do.

Remember, all successful resource boxes follow a three-step formula!

1. You make a huge benefit promise, or promise to avoid pain, usually in the form of a headline or opening sentence that grabs attention.
2. You support the claim in some way or build tension for avoiding the problem, usually with just a couple of quick lines.
3. Finally, you drive people to action by telling them "click here for <u>[fill in the blank]</u>".

Look at and learn from some examples of great resource boxes that do extremely well for myself and other people.

Study these resource boxes carefully and think about how you could adapt them to your own business.

<u>IMPORTANT NOTE</u>: You can, and should, always look to see what types and styles of resource boxes get published in a particular ezine you target. Look to see how wild, crazy and blatant the editor allows authors to get, or whether the editor tries to maintain

an overly professional tone. This will enable you to more effectively target your message for a particular ezine and you may find yourself mixing and matching articles and resource boxes to give yourself a better shot with a particular publisher.

** This resource box has done VERY well for us J

==================================

Why are some people getting rich selling their ebooks?

Jim Edwards & Joe Vitale have created the *ultimate* guide -

"How to Write and Publish your own Outrageously

Profitable eBook... in as little as 7 Days!"

FREE Details: ==> http://www.7dayebook.com

FREE Email-Course: ==> mailto:7dayebook@getresponse.com

==================================

Yanik Silver reports that this resource box has consistently performed for him for a couple of years now!

-=-

How Much Is One Good Sales Letter Worth To Your Business? Yanik Silver has created the ultimate no-brainer, fill-in-the-blank sales letter writing resource. In less than 3 minutes you can create a winning letter guaranteed to sell your product or service...

WITHOUT WRITING! Check out => Instant Sales Letters

-=-

Rozey Gean reports that when she started using this resource box her subscriptions and traffic increased dramatically!

-=-

Keep YOUR Publication and Online Content on the "Cutting Edge" with FREE content from Marketing-Seek. The place where smart Writers, Publishers and Online Entrepreneurs gather resources and build exposure.

M A R K E T I N G ~ S E E K . C O M

Web Site - http://www.marketing-seek.com/newsletter/
Subscribe - mailto:messenger@marketing-seek.net

-=-

We built this resource box out of the proven headlines we tested on the www.33daystoonlineprofits.com site.

=================================

How much would you pay to get day-by-day instructions from 2 top Internet marketing experts every day for 33 days? ** How about 88 cents? ** You can start with a few bucks and a good idea to make lots of money online! I did, and I'll teach you how no matter what product you sell...

Click Here => http://www.33daystoonlineprofits.com

=================================

This resource box did well for recruiting new subscribers to an autoresponder "mini-course"

-=-

Yanik Silver has developed a whole series of sales letter templates available at ==>Instant Sales Letters. In less than 3 minutes you can create a winning letter guaranteed to sell your product or service...WITHOUT WRITING! Or you can get more

surefire marketing secrets by subscribing to Yanik's free Ezine - just send a blank email

=> mailto: instantletters@getresponse.com

-=-

This resource box also came as a result of headlines tested on the sales letter website for the particular info-product (ebook).

==================================

Are YOU a "Lazy Achiever"?

"The Lazy Man's Guide to Online Business"

How to Work Less, get Paid More and have tons more Fun! Proven tips, tricks, techniques and strategies of Superstar "Lazy Achievers"!

Click=> http://www.getmoredonefaster.com

==================================

This resource box is a combination of a bio and a pitch that works well.

-=-

Jim Edwards, author of numerous best-selling ebooks, earns thousands in affiliate commissions every month! Jim has developed "Affiliate Link Cloaker," the easy, FAST, safe way to STOP affiliate link "hijackers"... Dead in their tracks!

Click Here => http://www.affiliatelinkcloaker.com

-=-

When an ezine editor wants a toned down resource box then I use something like this that sounds a bit more like a short biography paragraph, but is still basically a pitch for the book or product.

Jim Edwards is a syndicated newspaper columnist and the co-author of an amazing new ebook that will teach you how to work less, get paid more... and have tons more fun!

=> http://www.getmoredonefaster.com

Jim Edwards is the co-author of an incredible new ebook that will teach you how to write and publish your own highly profitable ebook in a week or less... even if you failed high school English class!

=> http://www.7dayebook.com

Jim Edwards is the co-author of a step-by-step, "paint by numbers" guide that guarantees to teach you how to go from zero to making real money online in about a month!

=> http://www.33daystoonlineprofits.com

Final Note on Resource Boxes:

Not every editor will publish your resource box exactly as you want it published. What do I mean by that? When some editors say they will publish your resource box, they actually mean that they will publish your short, non-promotional biography statement with a web link. Something like this:

Jim Edwards writes a syndicated newspaper column about current issues, problems and opportunities for non-technical people. "The Net Reporter" ==> http://www.thenetreporter.com

For a hard-core, overly-enthusiastic marketer like myself this rates about as exciting as eating plain, cold toast without any butter or jam – DRY!

However, though this type of "resource box" doesn't rate nearly as effective at making sales as having a resource box built on the "classified ad" model, sometimes you have to take what you can get.

Just prepare yourself mentally to come up with what you would rate as a "killer" resource box and then have a few editors replace it with your bio because they want to project a more "professional" image that doesn't blatantly pitch your product. <Sigh>

I know it can get a bit frustrating. But once you build up your announcement list where people ask to receive your articles — rather than you chasing them down and asking them — you can call the shots!

After you have formatted your article and created a compelling resource box you should post your article to your website…

Posting Your Article to Your Website

Once you finish formatting your article, create a compelling resource box, and put it into a text file, you really should post your article to your website. Why? So you can direct people to the article without sending the entire article to them.

Posting your articles to your site does a couple of very important things for you:

1. It gives you content you can refer your website visitors to and hold them on your site longer.
2. Each article gives you a "bridge page" the search engines can index and use to send you traffic.

An actual step-by-step "how to" for creating web pages, modifying them and posting them to your website goes beyond the scope of this ebook. That subject rates an ebook all by itself! I do, however, want to refer you to some sites that can help you learn how to post pages to your website… and the education won't cost you much, if anything.

Educating yourself about computers and software programs can represent a very expensive proposition in both time and money. Anyone who has ever seen those Video Professor advertisements on TV knows that a simple tutorial on CD-Rom costs $59 plus shipping and handling. Most people don't realize computer and software training is readily available online, some of it as good or better than the introductory courses that can cost you a lot of money.

Log on to www.findtutorials.com to find yourself in a world of learning about things that really interest you! Many of the tutorials listed come free of charge since the sites hosting the classes contain the usual advertising most of us have come to expect online. Some categories have more available classes than others, but the site rates a serious look and even a bookmark so you can check back for new jewels of knowledge on a regular basis.

Check here first before spending money on training, especially for introductory and general information instruction.

The following sites also offer free online training, however, understand that many of them use the introductory courses as a lead in to get you to purchase additional books, classes or other "advanced" instruction.

www.computertim.com

Offers an extensive collection of articles to help you learn how to operate various Microsoft Office programs more efficiently, including: the FrontPage web editor, Word, Outlook, Excel, and Windows.

www.lgta.org

Land-Grant Training Alliance – teaches you how to use various software packages online and even has an interesting tutorial on how to use the Internet as a teaching tool to help others.

www.trainingtools.com

Offers a variety of introductory training courses for software packages dealing primarily with website creation, installing scripts and making your website do cool things!

www.learnthat.com/courses/

Offers a variety of courses on everything from computer training and software packages to even dealing with some hardware issues and how to purchase the right digital camera.

www.elosoft.com/101/computer.htm

Offers a wide selection of links to other sites that offer online instruction, books, classes and other learning resources. Looks like an excellent place to start your search for additional information when you need instruction or help.

Creating a "Simple" Auto-responder

The final step before you start submitting your article comes by putting your article into a simple autoresponder.

You need to put your article into a simple auto-responder message because some article announcement sites and ezine editors require you to offer your article via auto-responder. Why? Because this enables people who want to read the article to request it via email, while others who don't want it won't need to read through it.

Having this set up ahead of time will save you an enormous amount of time when you start submitting as well as allow you to submit to a much larger audience.

We can't emphasize enough having this done correctly ahead of time when it comes to using submission sites to promote your article!

2 "Insider" TIPs on using Autoresponders:

1. You can also use these articles by autoresponder as the basis for a resource box or even as an ezine classified ad. Instead of putting your website at the end of the resource box, you put an offer for an article or a mini-course. As a good example, look here:

-=-

Yanik Silver has developed a whole series of sales letter templates available at ==>Instant Sales Letters. In less than 3 minutes you can create a winning letter guaranteed to sell your product or service...WITHOUT WRITING!

Or you can get more surefire marketing secrets by subscribing to Yanik's free Ezine - just send a blank email

=> mailto: instantletters@getresponse.com

-=-

2. You can also include information about one or two (or three) of your other, related articles in your autoresponders. At the top of the article that gets delivered by autoresponder you could simply put something like this:

Thanks for requesting the article, "Crying For Help Online" by Jim Edwards.

When you're done reading, check out this related article, also available by autoresponder:

Title: Cheap Web Hosting is NO Bargain!
mailto:cheaphost@33daystoonlineprofits.com

Use these basic steps to post your article into a simple auto-responder:

1. Format your article to 60 characters wide (following the directions in the previous section) so virtually anyone using any type of email program can open and read your message without funny carriage returns.

2. Insert your text at the top of the article offering another article or two on a related topic via autoresponder.

3. Log into the mail manager on your website, create a new user or mailbox name, and copy and paste your article into the autoresponder box.

   Here's how that process works with my web host – (Digital360)

a. Log into the control panel and select the "Mail Manager"

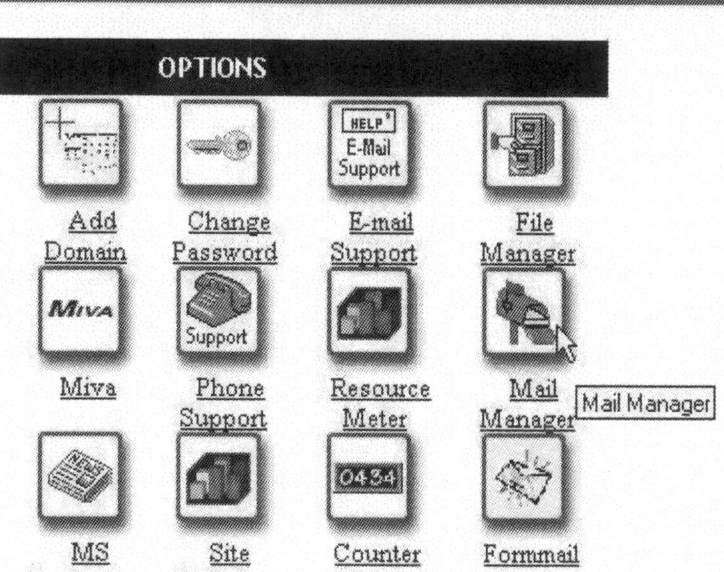

b. Set up a new email box with the basic name of your article Click "New Address" and then input the name you want for the autoresponder.

- Home
- Addresses **Max: 100**
  - answer
  - cheaphost
  - cryforhelp
  - howtheydidit
  - onlinepr
  - test
  - Default
- New Address

The "Input password" field is for using the mailbox as an actual send and receive email using a "Pop" box – so just put in something you'll remember, but don't worry about it for people getting your information via autoresponder. They don't need a password, they just need to send an email to the email address you create that offers the article.

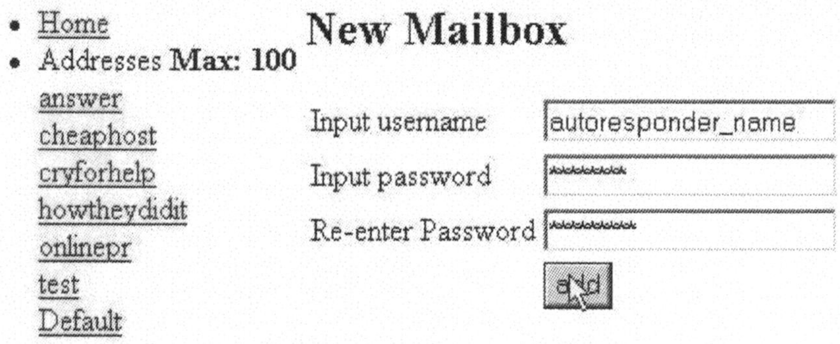

c. Paste your article into the autoresponder text box and click the checkbox to enable the autoresponder.

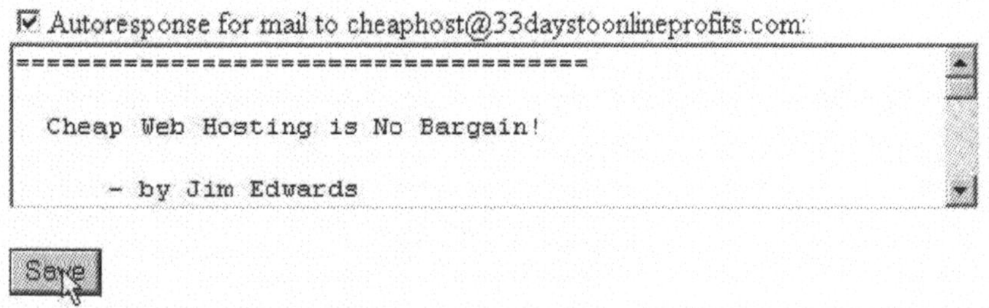

Special NOTE: Always distribute your autoresponder email address in emails and in articles using the mailto: format.

Example: mailto:cheaphost@33daystoonlineprofits.com

You do this so your email address will go live and "clickable" in almost every email program and website on which it shows up. Doing this rates as the email equivalent of typing in http:// at the beginning of every web address you send out.

By the way, most website hosting accounts now come with at least ten or twenty auto-responder accounts you can use for free, or as part of your

web hosting package. So, until you get up to ten or twenty articles, finding simple autoresponders shouldn't present a problem for you.

By the way, my friends at Digital360 give you 100 autoresponders with each website hosting account you set up.

You can also use this list of free auto-responder services to get yourself virtually as many autoresponders as you could need. But remember, anything free is worth what you pay for it. Free autoresponders almost always carry 3rd party advertisements and/or have little or no customer service support.

- **Get Response** – offers a free option, but all your messages contain 3rd party advertisements unless you upgrade to a "Pro" account.
- **Free Auto-Bot** – offers a free autoresponder that also allows you to send follow up messages automatically.
- **Send Free** – 3rd party driven advertising enables you to use their autoresponder.

OK! Now that you have your article formatted and posted to your website, your resource box done, an autoresponder, all your descriptions, keywords and other specific article information ready... let's move on to the point where the rubber meets the road – **submitting your articles to websites, ezines and article announcement sites!**

Specific Article Promotion Strategies & Tactics

How to market with your free articles and attract a stream of highly targeted visitors to your site.

SECTION 1:

General Principles Of How To Approach Other People To Publish and Post Your Articles

You can approach somebody to publish or post your article two different ways.

The first, send them a simple approach or contact letter, tell them about your article, why their readers might have an interest, and ask if they would like you to send the article. Or, if you're uncertain as to whether they accept articles, you might send them a quick email asking them if they even accept articles for publication on their website or in their ezine.

The second way, send the same type of approach letter along with the article in the body of the email itself.

IMPORTANT NOTE: One thing you should never do (unless specifically instructed to do so by a particular ezine editor or webmaster), DON'T send your article as a file attachment to an email message — no matter who you send it to! They will probably just delete your message and the attachment without even looking at it because of all the viruses rampant on the Internet today.

Another critical thing to remember: no matter whom you approach to run one of your articles, they get flooded with emails everyday. In order to have any chance of success, you must immediately tell them the benefits of "what's in it for them" by running *your* article as opposed to the many, many others they could choose.

If I had to boil down all the advice about approaching others to run your articles into three (3) steps, it would go like this:

1. **TARGET:**

   Make sure their audience is highly targeted for your subject matter. It does you no good to send Southwestern American cooking information to someone who publishes search engine promotion information. Don't expect anyone to run your article unless it hits on the wants, needs, desires and interests of their target audience.

2. **WIIFM** (What's In It For Me):

   Make sure you **approach them based on "what's in it for them"** and give them at least two or three benefits of running your article up front in your letter.

3. **PERSONALIZED:**

   Make sure to **structure your approach letter so it does not look like you decided to "Spam" the Internet** with the offer for your article. People hate "form letter" of all varieties. Make sure you use their name, their website and give some indication you know something about their business, their site or their audience. This can make all the difference.

Now, let's take a more in-depth look at specifically approaching various people who can run your article...

SECTION 2:

Promoting To Ezines Directly In Order To Get Them To Run Your Article

First, you should probably ask yourself this question: "Why would an ezine publisher publish one of my articles and send it to their subscribers?"

Think about it for a minute. ***Why would they*** publish one of your articles in their ezine or on their website?

The easiest and most obvious answer: **time**!

Everybody on the Internet stays busy all the time! People who publish ezines, particularly successful ezines, can't spend much time actually coming up with the content, especially if they publish every week. If you can provide quality content for their ezine, many publishers will use your articles and let you keep your resource box at the end to generate traffic and inquiries to your site.

Once you know they accept outside submissions, the number one way to persuade someone to run your article: Actually target their audience and provide them with highly pinpointed content for their main areas of interest.

Use these five examples of targeting an audience correctly to illustrate what I mean:

Example Target Audiences and Potential Subjects / Article Titles

For ezines and websites catering to Real Estate Investors

A. **"3 New Sources of Down payment funds"** – Investors always need money.

B. **"12 Fast / Easy Home Improvement Tips That Bring Back $100 for every $5 you invest."** – Investors always look for ways to increase their return without putting much money into a property.

C. **"5 Ways to Make Bankers Beg For Your Business"** – Investors often get snubbed by bankers, so they always want to know how to make bankers want to deal with them.

For ezines and websites catering to Amateur Gourmet Cooks

A. **"How To Save Money On Holiday Cooking Without Skimping On Quality"** – Everyone loves to save money... especially in a downward economy.

B. **"How to Get Free Cook Books By Starting Your Own Culinary Newsletter"** – show people how to get free stuff for taking easy action and you could have a winner.

C. **"How To Prepare A Gourmet Meal In Half the Time"** – Everyone loves to save time too!

For ezines and websites catering to Website Designers

A. **"4 New Sources of Free CGI Code"** – Free stuff gets attention.

B. **"How to Use Elance to Find New Customers – FAST"** – Any business owner wants to know how to get more business.

C. **"5 HTML Tricks that Cut Your Design Time In Half"** – Again, people love to save time.

For ezines and websites catering to "Newbies" (People new to the web)

A. **"How To Stop SPAM and Viruses At The Same Time"** – This is an actual article I wrote that still circulates widely online to this day.

B. **"5 Little-Known Sources of Free Computer Training"** – Free stuff!

C. **"Why Free Email Services Can Actually Hurt Your Business"** – Scaring people also rates as a great way to grab their attention and get them to read your article... especially if your product or service presents a solution.

For ezines and websites catering to Small Business Owners

A. **"How To Find High-Tech Help At Minimum Wage"** – What business owner wouldn't want to know how to get help in their business without spending an arm and a leg to get it.

B. **"Why Most Websites Fail... And What To Do About It"** – Again, fear gets people to read and most business owners fear failure.

C. **"Are Your Employees 'Goofing Off' Online?"** – Small business owners watch every dollar (at least the successful ones do) so they always want to know how to get the most for their money.

The moral of the story here?

Only approach ezine editors and website owners who directly cater to an audience your article targets. Why? Because if you do it correctly you can expect excellent results in traffic to your site and if you do it incorrectly you have just wasted an incredible amount of time!

Imagine an ezine publisher with 10,000 subscribers running your article as the featured article of the week. Not only will you get clicks to your site, but you will also build your reputation online with a huge number of people all at once.

Now, imagine that happening with a different ezine publisher every week. You can see how the clicks and the exposure start to add up with a compounding effect. If you structure your articles correctly with a killer resource box at the end, then the sales and subscribers also start to add up quickly.

Finally, imagine those same ezine editors running more of your articles over the coming weeks and months so you develop a virtual traffic machine that doesn't cost you a dime in advertising! VERY exciting!

So, the next question you should ask? "Specifically, how do I actually approach an ezine editor to get them to run my article."

Follow these steps:

1. **First, see if they even accept articles**. If a particular ezine does not accept articles, do not waste your time submitting to them. This may sound overly simplistic, but many people just blindly plow ahead doing it anyway, waste lots of time and then give up.

2. If they do accept articles, you must determine **what types of articles and subjects they want** and how they want them formatted. You do this by either visiting their site where they have their preferences posted or you email the publisher and ask for their article submission guidelines.

3. Next, find out how they want their articles submitted. If you submit the wrong way or inappropriately you just wasted your time because your submission will get trashed.

   Many editors now use forms or some other multi-step method to cut down on the amount of spam they receive from people blindly submitting articles via email. In fact, a number of software programs now on the market blindly and randomly submit to ezine publishers, making it extremely hard for you to get noticed over the noise of all the spam.

   You'll greatly improve your chances of getting your article published if you take the time to find out exactly how each editor likes to receive submissions and try to connect with them as a person rather than just a faceless email address you send your article to with reckless abandon.

   Side Note: Remember we told you earlier about your #1 objective of building relationships with as many ezine editors as possible?

Don't start off a relationship by dropping an avalanche of "spam" on them! You really only get one chance with each of these ezine editors... make it count!

4. Unless an editor requires submission through a form on their website, you just need to send them a brief approach letter with the article in the body of the message—not as an attachment. If you're unsure about whether they accept unsolicited submissions, then send the ezine publisher a brief note asking about their policy.

   Look at these examples of letters I've adapted and used successfully in the past.

NOTE: I just got off the phone with my friend, Yanik Silver, the publisher of "**Instant Sales Letters**." As I looked back over the letters I have successfully sent ezine publishers, I realized that the original letters I sent came from Yanik's "**Instant Sales Letters**!" I asked him if my dad and I could reprint those 2 letters here because I found them so helpful when I got started. Yanik very graciously agreed to let us give them to you.

Letter #1 – Ezine Editor Approach Letter *w/out* Article
(Courtesy of **Instant Sales Letters**)

> Subject: {first name}...question about submitting articles
>
> Hi {first name},
>
> I've been getting your {name} Ezine for some time now and wanted to ask what guidelines you had for article submissions.
>
> I've been published in {prominent ezine name} and {name} several times (along with dozens of other ezines).
>
> I really think your readers would enjoy and profit from the new articles I'm working on.

Thanks,

XXXX

P.S. If you want to see a few of my past articles - check out: {link to your article page}

Letter #2 – Ezine Editor Approach Letter *With* Article
(Courtesy of **Instant Sales Letters**)

Subject: {First Name} - New Article For Your Consideration

Dear {First Name},

Here is a new article for your consideration. I'm sure readers of your {ezine name} ezine will find the unique information from "{title of your article}" extremely useful.

Allow me a quick introduction. My name is {your name} and I'm the {author of or creator of ___(give a little background why you would be the expert_____}.

Please feel free to publish the article below along with my Resource box. Also, I'd greatly appreciate a courtesy copy when it goes out.

Thank you for the opportunity to contribute to your publication.

Best regards,

{Your Name}

{youremail@yourISP.com}

— Personal Details:

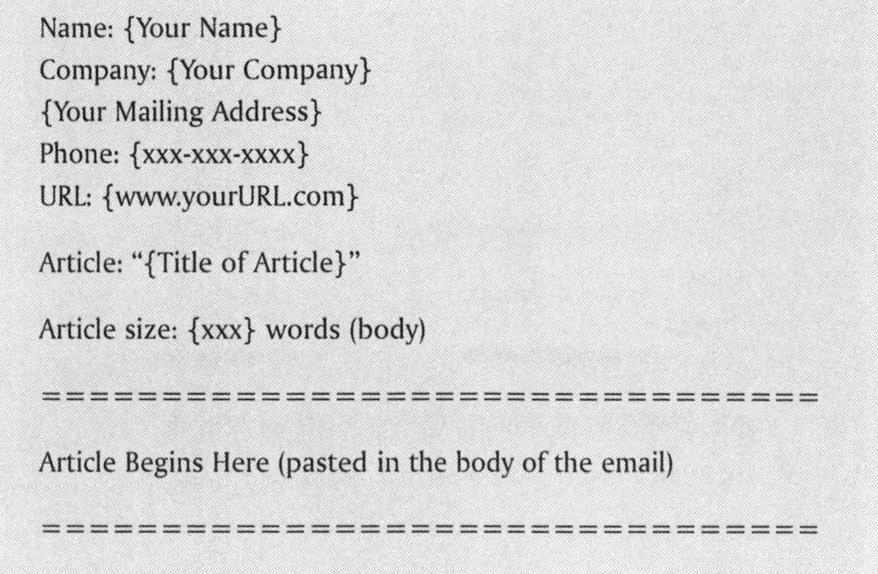

Name: {Your Name}
Company: {Your Company}
{Your Mailing Address}
Phone: {xxx-xxx-xxxx}
URL: {www.yourURL.com}

Article: "{Title of Article}"

Article size: {xxx} words (body)

====================================

Article Begins Here (pasted in the body of the email)

====================================

Letter #3 – Basic "Generic" Ezine Editor Approach Letter (If you've just started out this letter will give you the best example to use.)

Hi [[firstname]],

I am respectfully submitting my latest article in the hope that it will be of great interest to your ezine audience.

It provides insight about [[major benefit]] and also [[major benefit]] which I'm sure your audience will love since I'll bet they always want to learn more about

[[targeted subject of the ezine]].

The title is "[[title]]"

Please feel free to publish the article (at the end of this e-mail) including the resource box.

If you do decide to publish the article, would you mind please sending me a copy to let me know you used it?

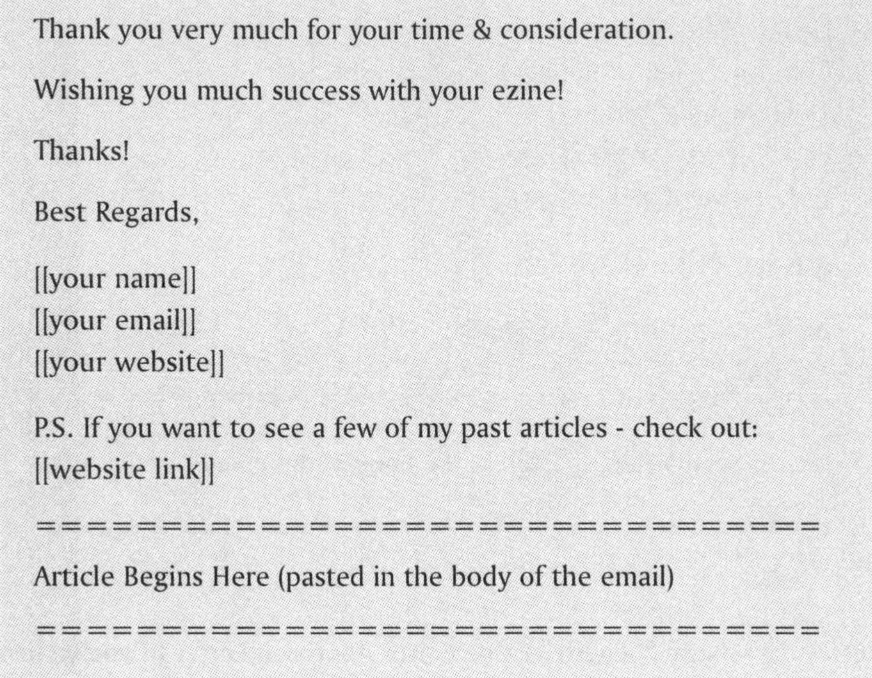

Thank you very much for your time & consideration.

Wishing you much success with your ezine!

Thanks!

Best Regards,

[[your name]]
[[your email]]
[[your website]]

P.S. If you want to see a few of my past articles - check out: [[website link]]

==================================

Article Begins Here (pasted in the body of the email)

==================================

Letter #4 – Ezine Editor Approach Letter Once You Have A Few Successes (But you can also adapt this style of approach even when you just start out with articles.)

Hi [[firstname]],

My name is [[your name]] and I'm writing to inquire about any specific and *immediate* needs you have right now for articles about [[their subject]] for your ezine.

I have written and published a number of articles on [[subject]] and have been published in [[related ezine]], [[related ezine]], [[related ezine]] and others.

All of my articles come from my front-line, "real world" experience of actually doing business online every day... so I can offer tips, tricks, techniques and information about [[subject]] your

[[Circulation number]] readers can use *immediately* and will reflect well on you as a publisher.

I regularly create original articles in the areas of:

~ [[area 1]]
~ [[area 2]]
~ [[area 3]]

Here are links to two articles I recently published:

~ http://www.article1.com
~ http://www.article2.com

Please let me know your specific article needs, how open you are to article submissions and how often (or not), as well as any other procedures you want followed for your ezine.

Thanks very much and I look forward to hearing from you.

Cheers,

[[your name]]
[[your site]]
[[your email]]
[[your phone]]

5. **START submitting your articles!**

   I hope by now you see that this procedure isn't complicated! You just need to take action… and now you will take action!

   Now you will go forth and find ezine publishers, send your article to those accepting articles and inquiring after those you don't know for sure.

One quick note before you charge off to find ezine editors.

I must tell you that the majority of the free directories that list ezine publishers require a lot of digging in order to find the information you need on publishers who can do business with you. Many of the ezine publisher listings in the free directories go out-of-date quickly or you don't know the size, circulation, age or quality of a particular ezine.

For this reason, I must highly recommend the "**Directory of Ezines**" which will cost you a few bucks for an annual membership, but you'll find it well worth the price!

"**Directory of Ezines**" allows you to sort through some of the most active ezines on the Internet to find the exact subject, circulation, publication frequency, determine whether or not they accept articles and sort through about a dozen other variables too. This resource makes it extremely easy to start finding ezines worth approaching and to avoid spending time on ezines that will get you nowhere.

Of course, with over 100,000 ezines online at any time, "**Directory of Ezines**" doesn't contain all of them, but they do maintain an excellent, up-to-date list that makes it extremely easy for you to quickly compile a list of targeted ezines and start submitting.

The following list of resources for finding Ezine Publishers is by no means 100% complete. Though it presents a number of resources, I know others exist. Also, from time to time, some of these links may go down. I will maintain a more up-to-date list online where you can get the latest list I have.

Just follow this link: http://www.turnwordsintotraffic.com/ezines/

Also, if you come across a great listing source for finding ezine editors I don't list here or on the website above, please drop me a line so I can add it. Thanks for your help!

Links to Ezine Directories to find publishers to run your articles

Please note: Not all of these resources will contain ezine editors for every single type of article you could write or every target audience. You will need to do some digging — especially in the free resources — to find ezine editors you can contact.

Directory of Ezines

The web's most up-to-date source for quickly finding editors who accept content. This will cost you a few bucks, but the time it saves you is worth its weight in gold!

http://www.turnwordsintotraffic.com/doe.html

Marketing Seek

Contains a neatly organized list of ezines by category and indicates in the list which ones accept article submissions along with editor and contact information.

http://www.marketing-seek.com/directory/index.shtml

Ezine Search

Searchable database of ezines you can look through to find publishers to contact about running your articles.

http://www.ezinesearch.com

Netter Web

Allows you to search by keyword for ezines that accept articles. Results do indicate the size of the publication and give the editor's email address and basic requirements.

http://netterweb.com/search/

Ezine Links

A very neatly organized site containing links to ezines... some of which accept articles.

http://www.ezinelinks.com

World Wide Lists

Offers a list of ezines - some of them quite large and well known. You will have to dig through and contact editors as it does not indicate which do and do not accept article submissions.

http://www.worldwidelists.com

Publicly Accessible Mailing Lists

Offers a searchable index of ezines and mailing lists they "guarantee" are as up to date as humanly possible on the Internet. You will have to contact each ezine and list publisher to find out their policies on accepting outside articles.

http://paml.net/

Ezine Universe

Offers an index of ezines searchable by category.

http://ezine-universe.com/

List Resources

Listings of ezines by category.

http://list-resources.com/

Ezine Investigator

Searchable database of ezines.

http://ezines.searchking.com/

Zinos

Offers a neatly organized directory of "hand-picked" ezines across the web.

http://zinos.com/

Ezines Plus

A site offering a select list of ezines organized by category.

http://ezinesplus.com/

The Ezine Directory

Offers a searchable database of ezines you can contact to see if the editors accept articles.

http://www.ezine-dir.com/

A List of Ezine Directories

Here is a list of lists of Ezine Directories.

http://www.writerswrite.com/epublishing/mldirectory.htm

Published.com Article Submissions

Links to editors accepting submissions. Does require some digging, but it is pretty well organized.

http://www.published.com/listings/submit.html

To find even more resources you should go to Yahoo! or Google and do a search for "ezine directories" as this will yield a whole lot of choices.

Now that you've found specific ezine editors to approach about publishing your articles, let's see about "announcing" your article so even more editors and website owners can find your work and put it in front of all their subscribers and visitors...

SECTION 3:
Promoting To Article Announcement Sites

Sorting through lists of ezines to find and contact editors individually uses a "proactive" strategy... sort of like a salesperson knocking on doors. Using article announcement sites acts as a "reactive" strategy... sort of like placing classified ads in the newspaper.

Article announcement sites offer websites ezine publishers and web-site owners can go to get content, usually for free, which they publish in their ezines or post on their websites.

With article announcement sites, you simply post your article, usually into a web-based form, or send it as an email message to a specific address. Either way, the article then gets posted onto a website or gets emailed directly to ezine publishers who placed themselves on a list to receive information about fresh articles offered with reprint permission.

Putting your articles onto announcement sites rates as an important promotion step, but not nearly as powerful as compiling and using your own list of ezine publishers and site owners who've published your articles in the past - but you still need to do it!

I personally post my articles to announcement sites during my "down time," usually in the evening or right after lunch when I can't do much deep thinking. Most of the time with announcement sites you can just

copy and paste information about yourself and your article into a web-based form.

Typically, article announcement sites will look for this information:

- ✓ **Title**
- ✓ **Author**
- ✓ **Author email**
- ✓ **Article url (address on your website)**
- ✓ **Autoresponder address for the article**
- ✓ **Article Word Count**
- ✓ **10 keywords describing the article**
- ✓ **20-30 description of the article**
- ✓ **Author's Bio**

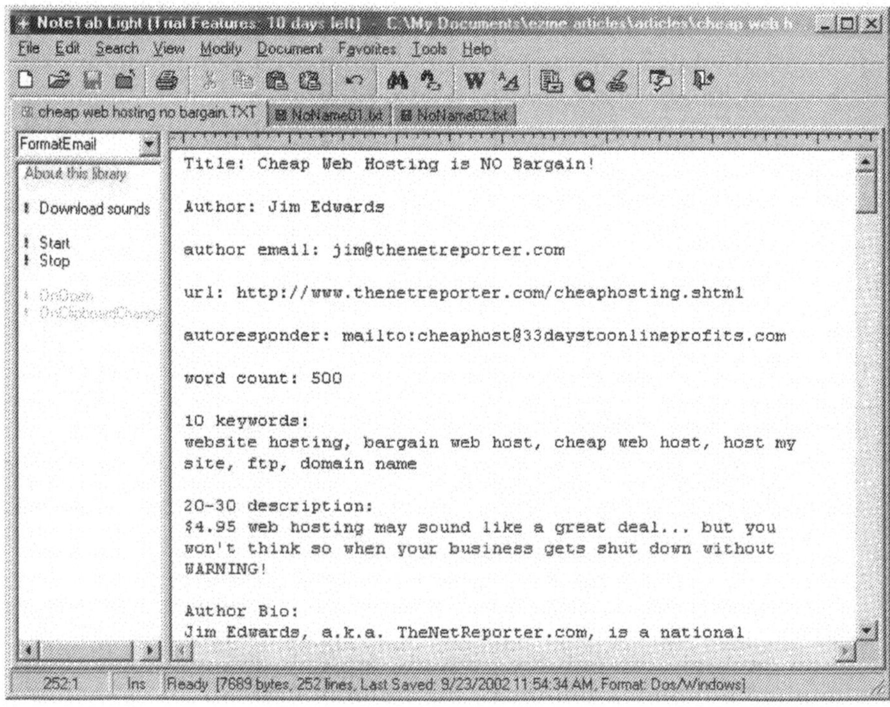

Some will ask for more, some less, but this covers the information the vast majority will ask you to provide. You will paste each of these bits of information into a different area of the form depending on what each particular site requires.

TIP: I always keep this information formatted ahead of time in NoteTab Lite so I can just copy and paste it into each form as plain text without any extra formatting or strange symbols that most word processors seem determined to include when you copy and paste.

Links to Article Announcement Sites Where You Can Submit Your Articles Right Now!

The following list of resources for announcing your site is by no means complete. Though it presents a number of resources, I'm sure many, many other sites exist. Also, from time to time, some of these links may go down. I will maintain a more up-to-date list online where you can get the latest list I have.

Just follow this link:
http://www.turnwordsintotraffic.com/announcementsites/

Also, if you come across a great source for announcing your articles that's not listed here or on the website above, please drop me a line so I can add it. Thanks!

Article Announce Writers and Publishers Exchange

Provides a number of lists for announcing your article to ezine publishers and website owners. One of the original sources online.

http://www.web-source.net/articlesub.htm

Author Connection

Allows you to contribute your articles to a searchable database where ezine publishers and website owners can search to find content matching their target audiences.

http://www.authorconnection.com

Idea Marketers

An excellent site for announcing your articles and posting them to the web.

http://www.ideamarketers.com

Ezine Articles

Provides a searchable listing directory for articles submitted by authors. Click "Submit Your Article"

http://www.ezinearticles.com

Marketing-Seek.com

Operated by my good buddy, Rozey Gean, this gives a must submit for your articles since many top ezine editors scan the archives when looking for new content.

http://www.marketing-seek.com

Netter Web

Submits your articles to a keyword-searchable database that ezine editors can browse for content.

http://www.netterweb.com/articles/

Publisher Network

A Yahoo Group where members can post articles by sending them as email messages to a special email address.

http://groups.yahoo.com/group/publisher_network/

Making Profit

Allows you to submit your articles to a free database searchable by web-site owners and ezine publishers.

http://www.makingprofit.com/

Go Articles

Provides a searchable database of articles and authors to which you can submit your articles for free. Their site "focuses on niche areas of particular interest to novices, webmasters, marketers, newsletter publishers, authors and entrepreneurs."

http://goarticles.com/index.html

Hot Launch

Maintains a searchable database of article listings on a variety of topics. Not a huge database, but it only takes a couple of minutes to submit.

http://www.hotlaunch.com/articles.asp

World Wide Information Outlet

Provides a searchable database of articles as well as the opportunity to have your content "syndicated" as a regular column appearing on other people's websites.

http://www.certificate.net/wwio/wglines.shtml

Select others:

Ultimate Profits

http://www.ultimateprofits.com/

ClickZ

http://www.clickz.com/submission/

Vector Central

http://www.vectorcentral.com/articles-form.html

Webmasters Library

http://www.webmasterslibrary.com/

Yahoo Article Announcement Lists

Visit each group to see how many members they currently have and how they accept submissions. These groups contain anywhere from a few members to hundreds of potential publishers who can post your content:

1. http://groups.yahoo.com/group/article-announce/
2. http://groups.yahoo.com/group/ArticlePublisher/
3. http://groups.yahoo.com/group/Free-eContent/
4. http://groups.yahoo.com/group/Free-Reprint-Articles/
5. http://groups.yahoo.com/group/FreeWrites/
6. http://groups.yahoo.com/group/freezinecontent/
7. http://groups.yahoo.com/group/netwrite-publish-announce/
8. http://groups.yahoo.com/group/publisher-network/
9. http://groups.yahoo.com/group/ReprintArticles-Paradise/
10. http://groups.yahoo.com/group/TheWriteArticles/

Another way to find announcement sites is to go to Google and do a search for "article announcement" or "article submission" and you can find additional sites.

Remember your ultimate objective here: to gather a list of people who have published your articles in the past so you can then directly email them your future articles. It may seem a bit time consuming in the beginning, but it will prove to be VERY worthwhile once you build your momentum.

SECTION 4:
Promoting Directly To Website Owners

Getting website owners to post your articles onto their websites will do a couple of things for you:

1. Create continuous exposure to a stream of traffic
2. Increase sales

I look at the process this way. If I can get 1,000 website owners to send me two visitors a day, that equals 2,000 extra visitors a day.

If I can convert 2 percent of those visitors into buyers then I make 40 extra sales a day. Does it always work out that way? No, but if you take on this mindset then you can see the power and value in working daily on getting more and more people to post your articles on their websites.

Take the easiest way to find people to potentially run your articles on their website by using a program like, "**Web Ferret**," "**Copernic**," or some similar search tool.

Do a search for your most popular keyword phrases as they relate to your target audience and look for the sites that come up related to that keyword phrase.

Save the searches and simply work your way down the list of those search results, contacting each of those site owners and asking them if they would like to run your article.

I'll show you a couple of letters I've used in the past after I show you an easy and organized way to quickly find hundreds of sites to contact.

This step-by-step tutorial will show you how to do just that using "**Web Ferret**" – a free program from Ferret Soft (http://www.ferretsoft.com).

> **Note to MAC users.** Web Ferret only works on a PC or a MAC running Virtual PC. If, for any reason, you can't use the program, you can always do various keyword searches on Google and then make notes in a spreadsheet of the sites you've already contacted.

Using Web Ferret

1. Install the program, which you can download for free from http://www.ferretsoft.com.

2. Make sure to set the program to avoid any duplication when sorting results.

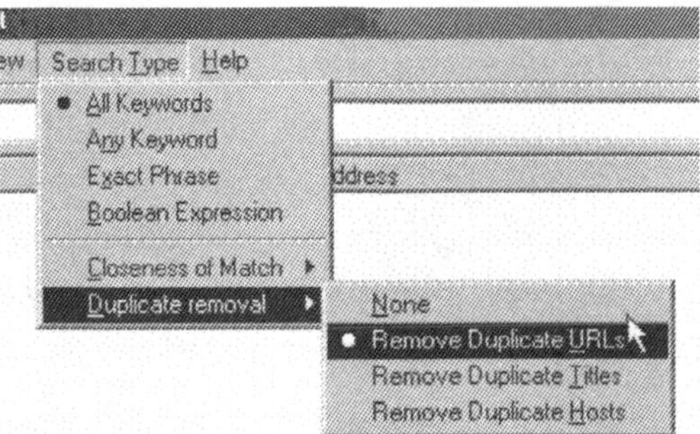

3. Reset the number of listings to gather from each search engine to 30 so you get the most sites. Also, check the box to automatically launch the search results in your browser once you're done.

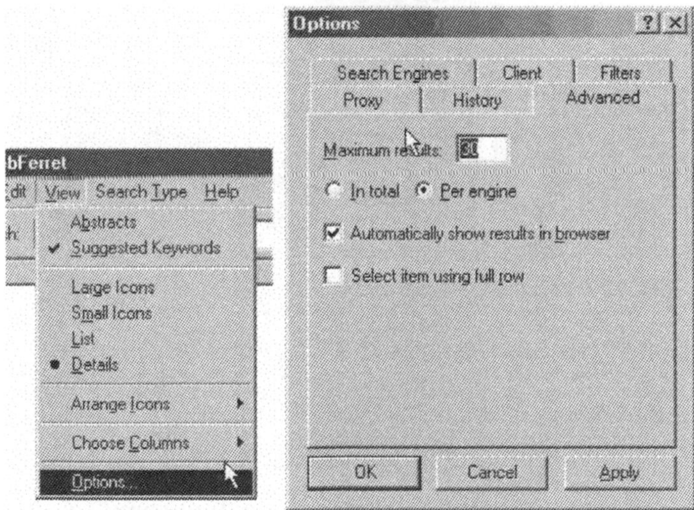

4. Do a search for your most prominent keyword phrase by entering the phrase and then hitting your "Enter" key.

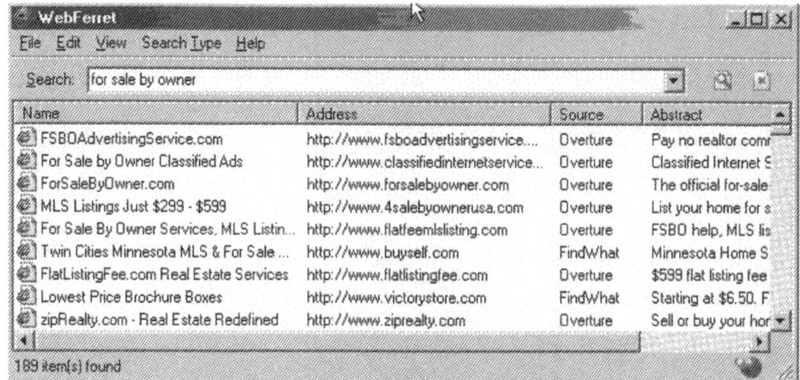

5. Ferret Soft will then launch a split browser window which shows the search results in the lower portion of the screen and the actual website you're looking at in the upper portion.

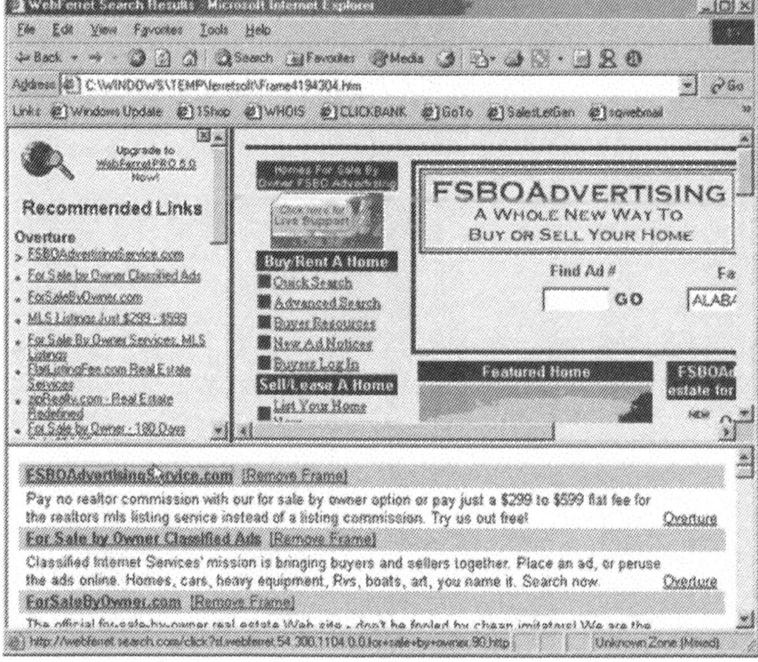

6. You then quickly make your way through the links selecting which sites to contact, browse each site to find and click on the site's contact email and send a brief letter. If you need to stop and come back later then save your search and make a note of where you left off so you can pick back up next time.

7. I keep track of the sites I contact in a spreadsheet in order to avoid duplication once I start doing additional keyword searches.

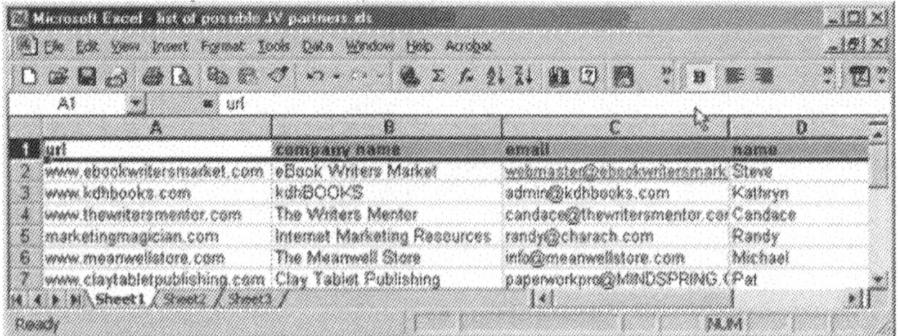

	A	B	C	D
1	url	company name	email	name
2	www.ebookwritersmarket.com	eBook Writers Market	webmaster@ebookwritersmark	Steve
3	www.kdhbooks.com	kdhBOOKS	admin@kdhbooks.com	Kathryn
4	www.thewritersmentor.com	The Writers Mentor	candace@thewritersmentor.co	Candace
5	marketingmagician.com	Internet Marketing Resources	randy@charach.com	Randy
6	www.meanwellstore.com	The Meanwell Store	info@meanwellstore.com	Michael
7	www.claytabletpublishing.com	Clay Tablet Publishing	paperworkpro@MINDSPRING.(	Pat

Specific tips on promoting your articles to website owners.

Make sure you actually contact sites worth contacting!

I use three criteria to evaluate whether or not to even bother contacting any site about my articles.

1. **Do they already post relevant articles written by other people?** If you find a site targeting your audience and they already run other people's articles, unless you insult them or their intelligence, you should persuade many of them to run your article as well. Websites matching this criterion definitely rate as your "A" list people.

2. **If they operate a newsletter from their site, then send an approach letter.** Simply ask them if they publish other people's articles or do special announcements. Since they already work with a large group (or even a small group) of your target audience, they probably need content.

3. **I see if they at least collect names in an autoresponder.** If they offer free reports or mini-courses to their readers this indicates they may need additional content. The upshot in this step means that you want to look for sites where they collect names and send things to people via email. This represents the best chance for finding someone who will put your information in front of their audience.

By following the step-by-step path I laid out in using "**Web Ferret**," once you work your way through one keyword search, you just do another keyword search until you've contacted as many sites as it takes to get the results you want.

To avoid duplicate submissions, I keep track of the URL, site name, email address of the owner, and owner's name in a spreadsheet. I can then sort the list by domain name to quickly see if I've already contacted a website owner asking them to run my article.

Here are two sample letters I've sent to website owners persuading them to run one or more of my articles. Please note that sometimes I just cut to the chase and ask website owners to run my article with their affiliate link in my resource box – especially if it looks like a busy site with lots of traffic. By doing this I have found a lot more of them say "YES" to posting my articles as opposed to someone else who doesn't make the same offer.

Regardless of whether or not you offer an affiliate commission in exchange for running your article, remember to clearly explain to them the benefits of running the article and how it will improve their relationship with their visitors by providing VALUABLE content their visitors will love.

Sample Number 1 — an email to a website owner who already runs other people's articles on their site.

> Subject: (author name) article on your site
>
> Hi [[firstname]],
>
> I'm writing you because I see that you have articles on your website written by (name), (name) and (name).
>
> I am respectfully submitting my latest article titled "[[article title]]" in the hope that it will be of great interest to your audience as it really complements the other articles you've posted.
>
> Specifically it [[major benefit]] and also [[major benefit]] which I'm sure your audience will love, especially based on the other articles I see posted.

Please feel free to publish the article (at the end of this e-mail) including the resource box.

If you do decide to publish the article to your website, would you mind replying to this email with the URL to let me know you used it?

Thank you very much for your time & consideration.

Wishing you much success!

Thanks!

Best Regards,

[[your name]]
[[your email]]
[[your website]]

P.S. If you want to see a few of my other past articles - check out: [[website link]]

====================================

Article Begins Here (pasted in the body of the email)

====================================

Sample Number 2 — an email to website owners who don't obviously post articles, but who operate a newsletter or offer free reports from their website via autoresponder.

Subject: [[firstname]], do you accept articles?

Hi [[firstname]],

I'm writing you because I see that you offer free reports / a newsletter / several autoresponders on your site.

I was wondering if you accept outside article submissions to include in your newsletter / autoresponder.

My latest article, "article title," specifically helps readers by [[major benefit]] and also [[major benefit]] which I'm sure your audience will love, especially based on the other information I see posted on your website.

Please feel free to publish the article (at the end of this e-mail) including the resource box. I've also included information about my affiliate program at the end, which by the way pays a handsome 50% on all purchasers you refer.

Feel free to substitute your affiliate link for my site link in the resource box.

If you do decide to publish the article to your website, would you mind replying to this email with the URL to let me know you used it?

Thank you very much for your time & consideration.

Wishing you much success!

Thanks!

Best Regards,

[[your name]]
[[your email]]
[[your website]]

P.S. If you want to see a few of my other past articles - check out: [[website link]]

==================================

Article Begins Here (pasted in the body of the email)

==================================

One more thing…

Before we leave this section, I want to you to visualize a high traffic website with 3,000 visitors a day publishing your article.

Imagine if you could get just one percent (1%) of those visitors to click on your resource box each day, that equals almost 11,000 extra visitors a year – from one source!

Now imagine having 100 sources just like it generate traffic for you.

That equals out to over 1 MILLION visitors a year!

See the importance of constantly looking for new sites and website owners to run your articles!?!

Believe me, the effort pays off in real money $$$$ and you should work daily on this activity.

SECTION 5:

Promoting Your Articles To Search Engines Using Free Online Tools

NOTE: This section assumes you have posted your article to your website.

Believe this simple truth about promoting your article with search engines: the rules search engines use to rank pages for various keyword searches change all the time. Unless you want to devote a significant amount of time to learning the intricacies and "voodoo" of getting pages ranked in the search engines, just do exactly what I tell you here and leave it at that.

You will achieve results with this simple technique. Instead of wishing, hoping and praying for an avalanche of traffic from the search engines, invest your time researching potential ezine publishers to run your articles or website owners to post them to their websites.

I only mention the search engines here because I get enough positive results with this technique to make it worth including!

After you post your article up to your website, you need to submit it to the search engines as quickly as possible and without spending any money on bogus search engine promotion services.

Make sure your article has properly formatted meta-tags included in the HTML code before submitting. I recommend just taking the one main keyword phrase and making that the first words in your title, keywords and description.

Example, if you write an article about “For Sale By Owner Selling Tips” then your meta-tags would look something like this:

<TITLE>for sale by owner selling tips</TITLE>

<META NAME=”DESCRIPTION” CONTENT=”for sale by owner selling tips article for sellers”>

<META NAME=”KEYWORDS” CONTENT=”for sale by owner selling tips”>

<META NAME=”REVISIT-AFTER” CONTENT=”30 Days”>

<META NAME=”ROBOT” CONTENT=”Index,Follow”>

You would then make sure that the first visible words on the actual page of your article were “For Sale By Owner Selling Tips”.

Now you have quickly done about 85% of what all those expensive search engine optimization courses teach you to do. As long as your article truly involves for sale by owner information, you should do okay in the search engines.

I have set up a meta-tag generator for you to use for free here in order to generate your meta-tags in the proper format. You can simply copy and paste the tags into your html documents:

http://www.turnwordsintotraffic.com/metatags1.html

Once you have prepared and posted your article it’s time to submit to the search engines.

Use these resources to submit the URL of your article and only spend about 10 to 20 minutes covering your bases with search engines. Again, you’ll achieve 85% of the results and you won’t spend 1/20th the time doing it.

- **Jim Tools** - http://www.jimtools.com/ – Click the "Submit Bot" section and you can submit your article to major search engines, directories and FFA pages.
- **Add Pro** - http://www.addpro.com/submit30.htm - submit your url to 20 top search engines including Google.

WARNING: **Do not submit the same page to the same search engine twice in one day!** This can get your entire website banned by the search engines. When using more than one automated service make sure you read which search engines they submit to so you can avoid accidental duplication.

SECTION 6:

Feeding Your Own Subscribers & Creating Mini-Courses

Feeding Your Own Subscribers

One of the most neglected areas for many online marketers, especially when they first get started, but also after they get "established," comes from spending the majority of their time thinking about how to acquire new customers and ignoring their existing customers. This will hurt you.

In truth, it rates five to ten times easier to resell an existing customer than finding and selling a new customer. One of the best uses for free articles to get traffic to your website, or another site through your affiliate link, comes with simply sending new articles to people who bought from you in the past or who signed up for your newsletter or mini-course.

Every time I release a new product, I always try to write one, two or a series of articles relevant to that product and include a resource box in each that directs people to the new website. For example: by providing fresh, free articles, I can take people who bought my 7-Day eBook and introduce them to my Affiliate Link Cloaker website. I simply created a useful article about how cloaking your links in your ebook helps you make up to 30% more money. This interested my ebook authors in reading the article and clicking through for more information about the software.

By using articles this way I do not send a blatant sales pitch, but I do provide useful information to existing customers. I show them I did not forget about them, give them something they can use, and do not constantly harangue them to make another purchase.

The same goes for people who signed up for my mini-courses and my newsletter. I can send them articles and gently, but effectively, push them to all the different sites I operate. I can take existing subscribers and turn them into traffic using articles, plus I continue to build my relationship with them and build value in their minds about my products by giving them great content with no strings attached.

The easiest, fastest way to distribute articles to your existing subscribers: Simply send an announcement to them through the sequential auto responder or list server you use to deliver your free reports and mini-courses already. Any good sequential auto responder enables you to send a broadcast email to all of your subscribers.

You would very simply introduce the article to them by saying something to the effect of:

> Hi first name,
>
> Jim Edwards here from ________.
>
> Based on information you've asked for in the past, I think you would be interested in this article I have written about __________.
>
> I just published it in my newsletter / or / it's been published by [[name]] in their newsletter, [[newsletter name]] and it details how to ____________.
>
> By the way, if you know of anybody else who would be interested in this article, please pass it along to them. If you publish an Ezine, feel free to publish this article or post it on your website. All I ask is that you leave my resource box intact.

I use these actual examples of different introductions when sending out articles to people on my various lists. As you can see, they get straight to the point and then direct the reader to do what you want them to do – read the article!

Hi [[firstname]],

Jim Edwards from www.7dayebook.com here.

Here is an article I just published in my ezine http://www.thenetreporter.com

Based on the fact that you are interested in writing ebooks, I thought the free tools I talk about in this article would get you excited.

Hi [[firstname]],

Jim Edwards from www.7dayebook.com here...

We thought this recent article about ebooks would interest you.

Thanks

Jim Edwards

www.7dayebook.com

Hi [[firstname]]

Jim Edwards from www.7dayebook.com here.

If you're having trouble finding the time to write your ebook - or accomplish any other "big" task for that matter—then this article I just published for my ezine may be just the ticket to help you.

Have a great day!

Jim Edwards

http://www.thenetreporter.com

Just give the reader a benefit or a self-serving reason to read your article and then get to it! They'll appreciate the brevity and you'll have a much better shot at having them read it.

Building Mini-Courses

You can also use articles to build value with your own subscribers and attract new ones by creating a mini-course where you put together three to five articles into a tutorial on how to get a certain result or how to avoid a specific problem.

A good example of a mini-course comes from one I offer at www.7dayebook.com. You can sign up for free by visiting the site and then reloading the page. A pop up window will appear to collect your name and email and then send you the first issue almost immediately.

I put four articles together and turned them into "How to Write and Profit from your own eBook... while you're still young enough to enjoy it!"

If somebody doesn't buy on their first visit to the site, when they leave, I offer this mini-course via an exit pop-up window. Thousands of people now subscribe to it and I feed them additional related articles regularly and sprinkle in occasional product offerings.

Regardless of whether you use the mini-course to reinforce your existing relationships with subscribers or attract new ones, a mini-course offers a much higher perceived value than a single article because, as a series of articles on a specific topic, you can cover more ground with people.

People love getting things of highly perceived value for free. So, a series of articles organized into a mini-course will increase their effectiveness as a means to get traffic to your site.

Take a look at this schematic (next page) for using a mini-course to funnel traffic around, not only to your own website(s), but to earn commissions as an affiliate as well.

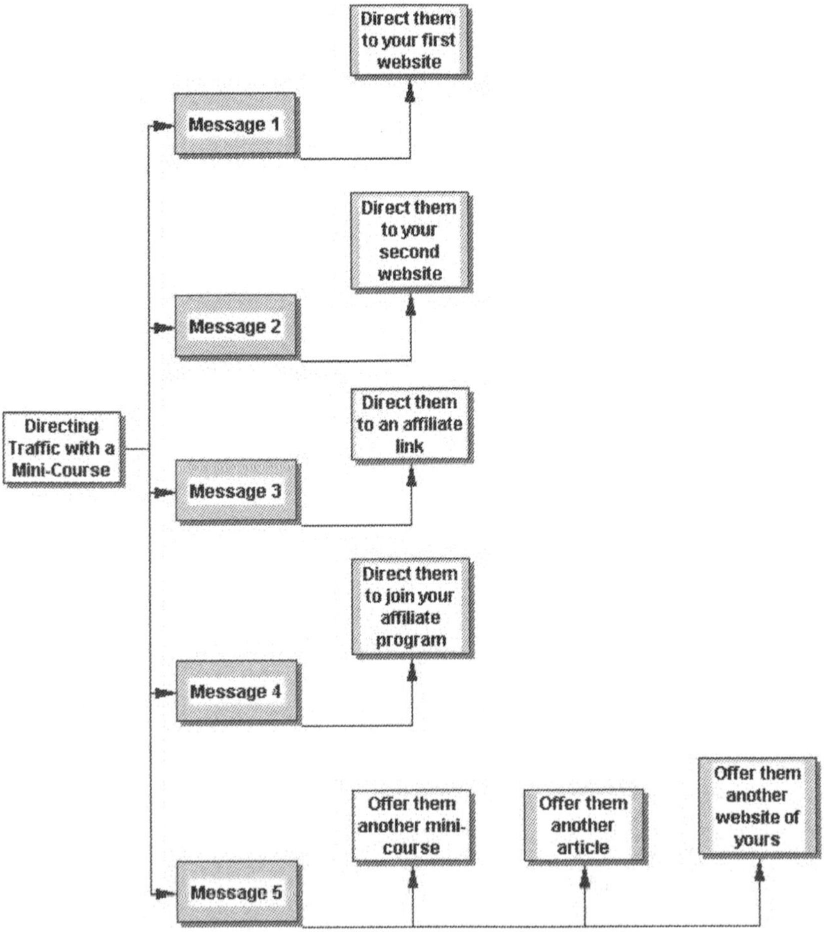

Directing Traffic with a Mini-Course

- Message 1 → Direct them to your first website
- Message 2 → Direct them to your second website
- Message 3 → Direct them to an affiliate link
- Message 4 → Direct them to join your affiliate program
- Message 5 → Offer them another mini-course; Offer them another article; Offer them another website of yours

By the way, another neat thing you can do with your mini-courses is allow other people to publish it in their own autoresponder and include their affiliate link wherever you would ordinarily post your website link. Any time they get somebody to sign up for the mini-course, instead of all the commission going to you, you share in it with them. Most importantly, by promoting your mini-course, they can add hundreds of people to your list and introduce thousands of people to your website very quickly in exchange for you giving up the short-term commission.

SECTION 7:

Put Your Articles In Your Affiliate "Tool Box" to help your Affiliate Build Their Business (And Yours)

When you have your own product and want to build your sales through affiliates, put articles on your website or in your affiliate "toolbox" and encourage your affiliates to use them. Doing so gives them the most valuable thing they can post on their website or publish in their ezine – quality content - and it can lead to significant sales for you.

Articles act effectively for affiliates in promoting, building, and proving the value of your product or service to their customers. They don't need to work hard in order to make money selling your product. If they can post an article on their website or send an article to their newsletter, they will make money without investing a lot of time in earning that income.

Once you write a great article with a resource box that pulls visitors and makes commissions, you need to give that article to your affiliates to use in promoting your products. If your affiliate software allows the use of custom fields you can even send the article to your affiliates preformatted with their affiliate link inserted in the resource box. All they have to do is copy-paste-make-money!

Study this example of an article I give my affiliates to use to promote one of my hot products as well as an offer to sign up to receive more articles automatically. Because I have my affiliates listed in an auto responder, I can automatically insert their affiliate link into the article. Literally, they only need to copy and paste that article into their newsletter or onto their website and they can start making money.

Pay close attention to the four main parts of the message:

1. Introduction
2. Offer of the free article service
3. The article itself with their affiliate link and ID automatically inserted
4. The reprint rights information at the end

> [FIRSTNAME], need quality content for your ezine / website?
>
> Hi [FIRSTNAME],
>
> Jim Edwards here with www.ebookfire.com
>
> Recently one of my best clients (who is also an eBook Fire affiliate like you) asked me:
>
> "Jim, I want to use some of your articles in my ezine, and in a couple of my autoresponder messages and put my affiliate link in your resource box. Would you mind if I did that?"
>
> My friend, David Garfinkel, and I decided to give this question some serious thought.
>
> We came up with a solution we think you'll like — because it's a virtually effortless way for you to send out valuable content (that you get for free) and make money on it (through affiliate sales).

It's called the Info Marketing Update (IMU) "Invitation Only" Article Service... and we'd like to invite you to participate!

Click here to sign up

=> http://www.ebookfire.com/articleupdate.html

Here's how it works:

1. You sign up for the IMU Free Article Service.

2. Then, two or three times a month, you get a fresh, money-making article ready to reprint in your autoresponder, in your ezine, or directly on your website.

3. At the end of each article is a resource box, with information about the author, and a link to a product.

4. Simply put your affiliate link in at the bottom — and you get a commission check for every sale that comes from this article!

The best part of this is, it's free, it's automatic, and there's no obligation! You choose only the articles you want to use, when you want to use them.

Click here to sign up

=> http://www.ebookfire.com/articleupdate.html

If you have any questions or need information on setting up your affiliate account, just send me an email.

mailto:jim@ebookfire.com

To Your Success,

Jim Edwards

P.S. To show you how easy this is and how profitable this can be for you, I've already included the first article with this email.

If you like, you can use this right away!

-=-=-=-=-=-=-=-=-=-=-=-=-=-=-=-=-=-=-

Creating Websites that actually make money!

- by Jim Edwards

http://www.thenetreporter.com

-=-=-=-=-=-=-=-=-=-=-=-=-=-=-=-=-=-=-

Not a week goes by that half a dozen people don't ask me what separates a great, money-making website from a bad one.

In response, I surveyed of a number of different websites, large and small, to find what they share in common to make them so successful.

With few exceptions, every extraordinarily great website contained the following elements.

~ Testimonials

Every great website has testimonials from satisfied customers. These testimonials help set the potential customer's mind at ease that the products or services sold online will perform as promised.

Truly great testimonials not only endorse the product, but clearly state how the product increased sales, saved money, or benefited previous buyers in very specific and tangible ways.

Testimonials should present real benefits others can readily identify with, understand and, more importantly, want those same results for themselves!

~ Headlines

Headlines capture visitors' attention and get them involved in the website.

How do you read the newspaper?

If you read like most people the headlines first catch your attention and determine whether you'll actually read a story.

Similarly headlines on a website determine whether visitors get involved in the information or surf away never to return.

My own experience has shown that the proper headlines can easily and quickly double, triple, or even quadruple a website's sales almost overnight.

~ Bullets

Bullets communicate various and subtle bits of information about a product or service without making readers plow through paragraphs of information to get to the meat of a website's offering.

Bullets arouse interest, build excitement and convey a lot of information very quickly to time-starved web surfers.

~ Bonuses

Every great website offers bonuses to people who buy, apply or fill out a form.

Nothing induces someone to do business with you online like offering them something extra for taking the action you want.

Offering a bonus report, tape, extended membership, extra quantities of product at a deep discount, coupons, or just about anything makes people more willing to go ahead with the purchase decision.

~ Guarantees

Everyone takes a risk whenever they buy anything from anyone.

The risk centers on whether or not the product or service will perform as promised. In a retail store most people feel pretty confident the store will still exist if they need to make a return or exchange in a few days.

On the web, however, that risk in making a purchase seems much higher than in the 'offline' world.

Every great website makes a point of specifically telling customers about their return policy and truly exceptional sites offer 100%, no-questions-asked, money-back guarantees.

People rarely take advantage of such guarantees and I have personally seen a website's sales increase by 45% just by extending the guarantee period an additional 30 days.

~ Phone numbers

Every great website has a phone number with a real live human being on the other end who can answer questions and provide product support.

So there you have it!

With few exceptions this represents the formula for creating or identifying a truly great website.

-=-=-=-=-=-=-=-=-=-=-=-=-=-=-

Jim Edwards, author of numerous best-selling ebooks, earns thousands in affiliate commissions every month! Jim has developed "Affiliate Link Cloaker," the easy, FAST, safe way to STOP affiliate link "hijackers"... Dead in their tracks!

Click Here => http://hop.clickbank.net/?[CUSTOM1]/ebksecrets

** Attn Ezine editors / Site owners **

Feel free to reprint this article in its entirety in your ezine or on your site so long as you leave all links in place, do not modify the content and include our resource box as listed above.

Feel free to substitute your affiliate link in place of our link in the resource box.

Earn up to 50% on every purchaser you refer!

Affiliate details are available here:

http://www.ebookfire.com

If you do use the material please send us a note so we can take a look. Thanks.

==================================

This email is *never* sent unsolicited.

Here is the information we have on record about your subscription:

Name: [FIRSTNAME]

Email: [EMAIL]

ClickBank ID: [CUSTOM1]

You, or someone using your name and email subscribed you to our "eBook Fire" affiliate program. If you feel there has been an error please click the link below to stop any future emails.

Use your articles to help your affiliates make you money! It only makes sense to do this as often as you can.

SECTION 8:

Taking Your Article Viral By Offering Free Reprint Rights

Another really great source of distribution comes from simply putting a tag line on the end of your article that says, "Hey, if you operate an ezine or a website feel free to use this article. Just send us an email and let us know if and where you used it."

Unless I have a specific reason for not doing it, I try to do this with virtually every article I publish and I get emails from people everyday saying, "Hi Jim, I just want to let you know I used this article in my Ezine. Thanks a lot, have a great day."

Many of those people publish it because they saw somebody else publish it, or they got it from me as one of my subscribers and at the bottom of the article it says, "Feel free to publish this article in your own Ezine."

Whenever appropriate, I always try to place this blurb of information at the bottom of any articles I send out.

> ** Attn Ezine editors / Site owners **
>
> Feel free to reprint this article in its entirety in your ezine or on your site so long as you leave all links in place, do not modify the content and include our resource box as listed above.

Feel free to substitute your affiliate link in place of our link in the resource box.

Earn up to 50% on every purchaser you refer!

Affiliate details are available here: http://www.ebookfire.com

If you do use the material please send us a note so we can take a look. Thanks.

As with anything of this nature, watch for a couple of pitfalls with letting people reprint articles without asking permission first. I need to make you aware of them, but don't let them discourage you from using this technique.

- First, every once in a while people who run your articles will change your resource box or they will take your resource box off the article completely. This doesn't happen very often and it should not stop you from using this strategy.
- In extreme (very extreme) cases, you may find that somebody actually steals your article and puts their name on it. While very rare, people can do that in the offline world too. You just need to stay aware of the possibility, but you can do some things to protect yourself.

First, clearly spell out the rules for allowing them to reprint your articles. The rules can rate as simple as one paragraph like this:

** Attn Ezine editors / Site owners **

Feel free to reprint this article in its entirety in your ezine or on your site so long as you leave all links in place, do not modify the content and include our resource box as listed above.

Or you can get a bit more formal and specific depending on how much you want to control people's use of your material

David Garfinkel and I (Jim) use these rules to let people know our terms right upfront before they even see the "Article Archive." Doing it this way prevents a lot of the funny business people tend to get into if you don't lay down the law right up front.

These articles provide excellent content as well as money-making opportunities for you in the resource boxes.

We have 4 Ground Rules - and if you use any of these articles then that is explicit and implicit agreement on your part to these rules:

1. **We retain all copyrights and credit for writing these articles** and you may NOT claim, assume or infer any copyright, authorship, or other rights to the content in any way.

2. **You MUST include our resource boxes** at the end of the articles with a link back to the specified site. You are welcome to insert your affiliate link in place of our website link.

3. **Any article you publish must be published in its entirety.** You may not publish the articles in pieces or in sections or as part of an ebook without expressed written permission of the author(s).

4. **You must NOT publish any of these articles in an ebook** or any other collective work (online or offline) without the expressed written permission of the author(s).

You can use these rules, modify them, or come up with your own and post them right on your own site or even include them with your article if it makes you more comfortable.

SECTION 9:

Develop Your Own "Article Announcement" List

By creating and growing your own article announcement list you literally get hundreds and then thousands of people waiting for you to write articles so they can publish them in their ezines or on their websites.

Developing your own Article Announcement list offers one of the most powerful strategies you can adopt, but you can really only use this if you plan to publish your own articles on a regular basis.

With your own article announcement list you can literally create an avalanche of new visitors every time you publish a new article... you only need a sequential autoresponder and some basic html skills.

Jim and his co-author on "eBook Secrets Exposed," David Garfinkel, operate an article announcement service at http://www.infomarketingupdate.com/archive/ where just about every week or week and a half, subscribers get sent a new article they can run in their ezine or post on their website. A side bonus to this article announcement service: it lets all of the people who subscribe also read the articles... and some of them buy from the resource box as a result!

What's the greatest thing about operating an announcement list for our own articles? Simple. Instead of going out to find people to run our articles, they come to us! We simply say to people, "If you need quality

content for your ezine or website, click here to get fresh content delivered right to your 'in-box' on a regular basis."

People know us, our reputation, and our ability to provide good content. They just sign up, give an email address and they immediately get access to our archives. Since the service works around a sequential autoresponder, by signing up they will automatically start getting regular announcements whenever we publish a new article.

Once you put together five or six articles, you can then set up your own archive area. You do not need special software to do it, you just need to know how to post basic web pages to your website and you can create an archive. Then you need a simple sequential autoresponder that can broadcast to all your subscribers and away you go!

I recommend **Get Response** as the simplest and easiest sequential autoresponder to use.

You set it up so that people who like your articles can receive and reprint them as you email the articles.

We've set ours up so that subscribers get 4 messages automatically no matter when they join and then start getting the periodic updates when we release new articles. The following represents the actual sequence we use in our very successful article announcement service.

You can model your article announcement service on these steps if you choose. Specifically I want you to notice how we train people to use our articles to make themselves (and us) money by teaching them how to introduce the articles to as many people as possible.

1. **Message 1 – Welcome Message [sent instantly]**
   a. Explains the system we've set up
   b. Tells them how often they should expect articles each month
   c. Tells them where to find new articles in the archive (URL)
   4. Encourages them to go grab an article right now and publish it.
2. **Message 2 – Article Tip #1 [sent 7 days after signup]**

a. Reminds them where to find articles in the archive (URL)

b. Gives them a valuable tip on how to introduce the articles to their lists and website visitors to increase readership.

3. **Message 3 – Article Tip #2 [sent 14 days after signup]**

   a. Reminds them what they signed up for (our article service) and why they signed up (to get great content free they can use to make money).

   b. In this week's tip we encourage people to put our articles into their autoresponders so they go out automatically.

   c. We remind them that they can always go over to the archive and grab a fresh article any time they need one.

4. **Message 4 – Article Tip #3 [sent 21 days after signup]**

   a. Reminds them what they signed up for and why. This repetition cuts down on un-subscribes and also reinforces the motivation that caused them to sign up in the first place!

   b. The message motivates the reader to do something. It shows them how most people sign up for a service but then never do anything about it! We encourage them to go grab an article and do something with it.

   c. We remind them where and how they can get articles any time they need them.

5. **Message 5 – We ask for article requests [sent 28 days after signup]**

   a. At this point, hopefully only motivated people who will run our articles are still on the list. We ask them if they have any specific article requests or suggestions for article topics.

      i. We always try to send a thank you note to whomever sends us the article suggestion.

ii. If we already have an article that meets their needs we direct them to the archives or we email them the article.

iii. If we don't have an article, but like the idea, then it goes into the idea bank and eventually we write an article on it.

iv. If we don't like the article idea then we don't do anything with it.

This flowchart represents the process for quickly building up your own list of people who want to publish your articles on their websites and in their ezines.

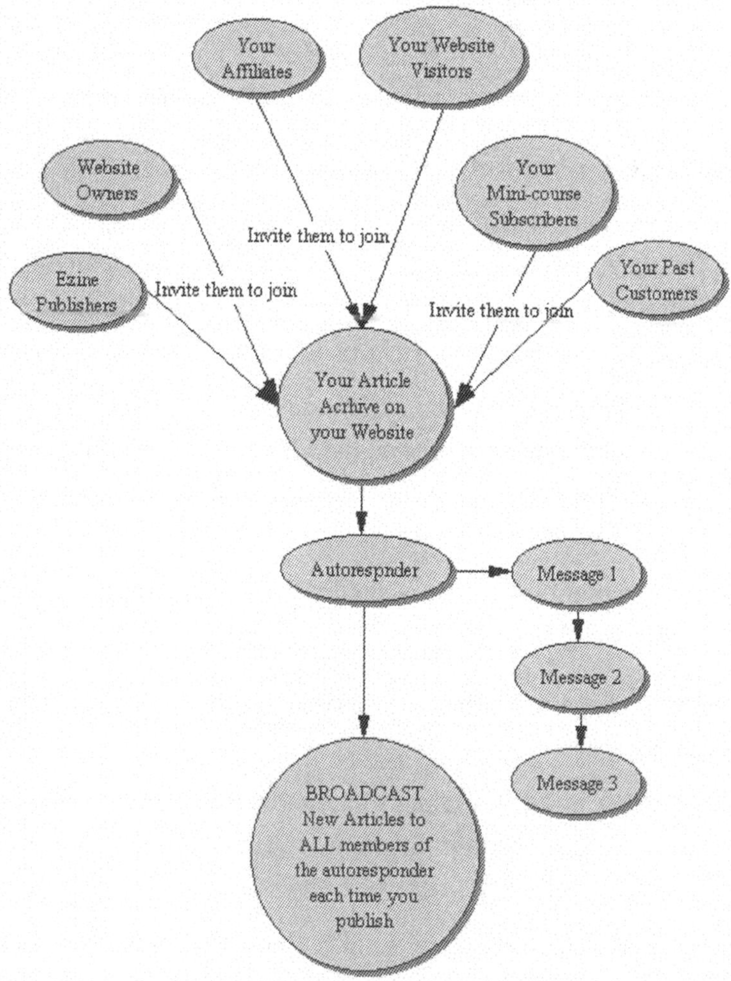

The best way to get subscribers in the beginning involves just inviting anybody who runs one of your articles in their ezine or posts your article to their website to sign up. Simply ask them, "Hey, since you liked this article enough to run it, would you like me to automatically notify you each time I publish a new article?"

Many of them will say yes and then the process just builds upon itself as you add more people to your list over time.

SECTION 10:

How To Market With Articles Even If You Can't Find Time To Write Them Yourself

After reading everything we've written here in this ebook so far, you may decide you can't find the time to write your own articles; however, you do understand that promoting with articles provides a very, very powerful means of getting visitors to your site. What should you do?

Well, consider two things you can do.

First - Simply log on to http://www.elance.com and hire somebody to write an article for you.

Commonly referred to as "Ghost Writing," many people will write a decent 500- 600 word article on any topic you specify for between $50 and $100. Once the article gets written, you spend your time promoting the article. Post it on your website, run it in your autoresponder, approach other people to run it in their ezine and post it on their website just as if you wrote the article yourself.

> NOTE: Make sure when you hire someone to write the article for you that it gets done as a "work for hire". This means you own the article and can do whatever you want with it. You should go ahead and put your name on the article as the author – you own it!

When hiring someone to write your article for you, follow these tips to help ensure a better experience:

1. Make sure they fully understand the subject you want them to write on and won't just "wing it" because they need the money.

2. Ask to see samples of their past articles so you can see their writing style and measure their level of professionalism.

3. Look at the feedback they have received from their past clients and look for any patterns that indicate a decline in their service level or their inability to deliver what they promise.

4. Make sure they understand you own the copyright to the article and can do as you wish with it, including putting your name on it and claiming authorship.

5. Don't hesitate to ask for revisions or clarification to the article before accepting delivery of it.

6. Explore the possibility of their writing a follow-up article right then on the spot at a reduced rate.

By far this represents the best strategy if you don't have the time to write your articles yourself.

The second way to market with articles when you don't have enough time to write them yourself: Go find other people's articles and put them on your site with your affiliate link in their resource box. You also can take those articles and try and find other people to run them (leaving your affiliate link intact). I will tell you quite honestly you will find this a tougher road to travel, but you can do it!

To give yourself a better shot at making this second technique work you should "cloak" your affiliate link so readers and potential publishers can't immediately tell you've used an affiliate link.

Instead of putting a link like this into the resource box – http://hop.clickbank.net/?ezarticles/cloaklinks

You would use a link that looks like just another page on your website http://www.turnwordsintotraffic.com/cloak.html

They both take you to the same page, but one looks more "legitimate" than the other.

> NOTE: You MUST read the reprint instructions and restrictions placed on any third party articles you use to make sure the author doesn't prohibit you changing their links to your affiliate link or distributing their articles to other parties. If you are in doubt ASK the author of the articles before proceeding!

SECTION 11:

Additional Creative Uses With Articles That Can Make You Money and Save You Time

1. **Use your articles as bonuses when selling a product: either your own, or somebody else's.**

One of the important ways you persuade people to purchase your products and other people's products comes from offering bonuses. You can come up with a bonus really fast by taking an article, elaborating on it, making it longer, and then calling it a "Special Report".

This technique works really well not only with your own products, but also by "sweetening the pot" when you offer your subscribers someone else's product through your affiliate link.

For example, let's say you endorse a software product that allows people to conduct surveys of their website visitors. As a bonus you could offer various articles about how to choose which questions to ask, how to increase response rates, the TOP 10 reasons to conduct a survey, and how to use the survey results to make yourself more money. You could then make those bonus articles exclusively available only to people who purchased through your affiliate link and send you a copy of their receipt

Piling on the bonuses almost always helps sell more products.

You can also cut down on returns by giving people a stream of "unadvertised" bonuses which you send them once a week for four or five weeks. Articles make excellent "unadvertised" bonuses. The types of articles you use as bonuses, unadvertised or otherwise, normally get more in-depth into a certain subject than you cover in the actual ebook or product itself.

For example: With the "**Lazy Man's Guide to Online Business**," we use four unadvertised bonuses given out once a week for four weeks on these subjects:

1. **"CLARITY" - a Major short-cut to a "Lazy Achiever's" Online Dream Business.** How to get really clear on what you want.

2. **The "Lazy Man's" Guide to Handling Customer Problems and Complaints** - "How respond to your customers to create long-term positive relationships using the lazy man's principles for handling problems - large or small."

3. **The "Lazy Man's" Guide to Motivating yourself into Action!** "How to 'light a fire under your feet' so you can get the most done... with the least effort... in the shortest time possible."

4. **The "Lazy Man's" Guide to: "Never Underestimate or Pre-Judge Anyone... Online or Otherwise!"** – How prejudging people and situations can hurt you and your profits.

Each of these unadvertised bonuses provides additional information not covered in the book, and each of them started out as 500 word articles. We simply expanded them to make them a little "meatier," packaged them up as "Special Reports," and put them in a sequential autoresponder so people who buy the book automatically receive them once a week for 30 days following a purchase.

2. **Using articles as a "bribe" to complete a survey, either yours or other people's.**

Without a doubt, one of the most powerful marketing tools anybody can use involves an online survey. Surveys help you find out:

- What information people want from you
- Why they do and don't subscribe to your newsletter or mini-course
- What they want to buy from you and from other people
- What they will buy next
- What they are willing to pay for the things they will buy
- … and just about anything else you want to know about your target audience.

The challenge with surveys always comes back to the fact that busy people need a **reason** for actually taking your survey. Why should they bother doing something for you unless they get something in return for taking action?

You can use articles very effectively as bribes to get people to take a survey as long as the article interests them. You will massively increase the percentage of people who take your survey by anywhere from **three to fifteen times** by simply offering an article in exchange for taking the survey.

Purchasers of my "**How to Write and Publish Your Own eBook… in as little as 7 Days**" all receive the following survey that offers articles as a reward. By the way, as a result of using these free articles, thousands of people responded to this survey. The marketing intelligence we gathered increased our sales by an extra $50,000 because it enabled us to focus in on exactly what our customers wanted and give it to them.

> [[firstname]] - 2 minute survey + Free Gift
>
> A Free Gift in return for your help!
>
> Hi [[firstname]]
>
> Jim Edwards from www.7dayebook.com here.
>
> I'm working on a new project that should take ebook writing and marketing to the "next level".

Rather than guess what people want, I decided to ask you—someone who is interested in writing, publishing and selling ebooks.

==> A FREE Gift (bribe) for you!

Below is a short survey - it should only take you about 2 minutes to complete and email back.

As a thank you (*bribe*) for filling out the survey I will send you a FREE Gift — two interviews I did with two of today's top Internet Marketers: Yanik Silver and Danny Sullivan.

(You will *love* this one!)

Yanik Silver talks about how he got started with his Ultra-successful Instant Sales Letters website and how he went from zero (0) to over $100,000 a year in less than 12 months!

Danny Sullivan—the original search engine guru—drops some great nuggets of wisdom about using search engines to promote your site!

You sure won't find these interviews anywhere else on the web for free!

Once you return the survey I will send you the articles personally (since I won't be sending them by autoresponder it may take an hour or two in between checking my mail... but I *will* send them to you)

Please take *two minutes right now* to fill out the survey and you'll get a couple of very informative articles for your time.

Thanks in advance for your feedback and help.

Jim Edwards

Co-author "How to Write and Publish your own eBook... in as little as 7 Days" http://www.7dayebook.com

==========================

Ebook survey

Directions: Just hit your email "reply button" make "X" marks in between the [ ], fill in numbers, or answer Yes or No as indicated in each question.

Then "send" the survey back to us.

1. Please rank these in order of importance (1,2,3,4,5) with #1 most important, #2 next most important, etc.

[ ] Learning how to get more prospects to your website (traffic)

[ ] Learning how to make more money from each book sale

[ ] Learning about systems / software for ebook delivery

[ ] Learning how to create a stream of "passive" income

[ ] Learning advanced techniques for how to create ebooks quickly

2. Which would you be most likely to buy in the next 6 months (X in each box that applies)

[ ] Ebook "compiler" software (makes "ebooks")

[ ] Advice on Ebook marketing

[ ] Advice on pricing ebooks

[ ] Advanced techniques for selling more ebooks

[ ] Advanced techniques for creating ebooks quickly

[ ] Other: (fill in here)

3. Ebook software

Would you be interested in Independent Reviews of various ebook software creation programs.

[ ] (Yes / No in the box)

If "yes" - How interested? (X in the box)

[ ] Very Interested

[ ] Interested

[ ] Slightly Interested

4. Ebook delivery

Would you be interested in step-by-step, "paint-by-numbers" instruction on how to set up a totally automated ebook delivery system on the web?

[ ] (Yes / No in the box)

If "yes" - How interested? (X in the box)

[ ] Very Interested

[ ] Interested

[ ] Slightly Interested

Thanks for your input. Please email this survey form back along with your name and email to:

Jim Edwards at mailto:info@7dayebook.com

I will send you your FREE gift for taking the time to fill out the survey.

Jim.

3. **Use articles to expand an ebook or info-product – either your own or somebody else's**

You can use articles as filler or as elaboration on a specific topic in your own ebook or somebody else's. I do this repeatedly, especially when the existing article really covers a specific point in a lot of detail. It saves me a lot of time and I even did it in this ebook in several spots!

You simply insert the article directly into the ebook at an appropriate spot and either tell people, "Hey, this article covers this subject very thoroughly. Enjoy!" or you just blend it seamlessly into the text.

We also used this technique extensively in the "**33 Days to Online Profits**" course. We included numerous articles in the text at strategic points when we wanted to elaborate on a particular day's lesson, but it didn't really fit to include the article text as part of the chapter itself.

Look at how we did it.

On page 17 of "**33 Days to Online Profits**," we offer people 2 articles at the conclusion of the first day that, though they contain important information, don't really fit in the chapter text itself. So we just include them at the end with this introduction:

> We have two feature articles for you today:
>
> - The first will help you evaluate your current Internet skills...
> - The second will help you avoid one of the most common pitfalls many new online business owners encounter.

Then we just inserted the articles in the ebook and kept on moving!

4. **Compile groups of related articles into free or low-cost ebooks.**

Normally, this works best for a free ebook. If you write (or own) ten or fifteen articles on a specific topic, say "E Commerce," you could put them all into an ebook, call it "E-Commerce 101" and give it away to people in

exchange for their signing up for your newsletter, use it as a bribe for taking your survey, etc.

This very simple technique can give you an ebook with enough perceived value that you can leverage it as a "freebie" very easily. But, you better have some hard-to-find *valuable* information if you want to simply compile a group of articles into an ebook and try to sell it without first piling in extra value.

The easiest way to create an ebook with your 10-15 articles involves just putting them together neatly in your word processor and then converting them into a PDF (Portable Document Format). Users read PDF files through the free Adobe Acrobat Reader program. Using this file format also makes your ebook accessible to both PC and MAC users.

Just take your articles and insert the following elements to add perceived length and give it the feel of an "ebook":

1. Title page
2. Author bio
3. Foreword about your website or an offer for your FREE mini-course
4. Table of Contents
5. Introduction
6. The 10 – 15 articles each listed individually by title as "chapters"
7. A conclusion
8. Additional resources

You can compile 5 free PDF documents by converting your word processing files at this website: **http://createpdf.adobe.com**

5. **Increase your "Link Popularity" in the search engines.**

Look at this hidden benefit and motivation for carrying your articles on a whole bunch of other people's websites. This can increase your "link popularity" with the search engines without your doing any search engine promotion.

Now many of the search engine "gurus" and purists out there "know everything" about search engines. They will say that this linkage will show as duplicate content and the search engines may penalize you. I disagree! You can go to Google and put in names like "David Garfinkel" and see hundred's and thousand's of links come up. Most of them come about as a direct result of a dozen or so different articles.

So, promoting with articles on other people's websites directly relates to the side benefits of increased link popularity... without you having to do anything extra for it!

6. Making Money with "Sleeper" links

I saved this for last because it rates as my absolute favorite "secret" strategy.

A very creative use for making money with articles, uses what I call "sleeper" links in the actual text of the article.

Whereas people looking to run your article will look primarily at the resource box as a most important way for them to make money, people who read your article will sometimes look at the resource box somewhat suspiciously. They know about your commercial intention behind that very enticing and motivating resource box and may remain a bit skeptical.

However, if you can find a way to insert money-making links into the actual article itself, then this can help generate a significant income without arousing the suspicion of the publisher or the reader.

There are a few different types of "sleeper" links you can use in your article.

> NOTE: Make sure you don't use or abuse these techniques in an underhanded fashion because doing so will cause ezine publishers and site owners to "blacklist" you and not want to run your articles

in the future. Use them honorably and they should help you make additional cash!

Sleeper Link #1 – The "Example" Link- With this type of link you offer to illustrate the point, show proof, or otherwise clearly demonstrate an example of something you detail in your article. In this case, below the link takes the reader to my affiliate link for someone else's product as a demonstration of the technique I'm explaining in the actual article.

Example from an actual article:

> The first and cheapest way to hide your affiliate links is using a java script refresh page. This is where you hide the link in a page on your site that redirects people to your affiliate link using a simple java script.
>
> It works great not to expose your naked affiliate link in your actual email messages and ezine ads, but once people get redirected to the true link many affiliate programs expose the affiliate link with your ID in the browser address bar.
>
> Here's an example of a redirect script in action.
>
> Click => http://www.ebookfire.com/bfl.html

Sleeper Link #2 – Get a Free Script (or anything else) Link – With this type of link the reader will get something for free if they click over to the link you give them. Since the link represents an integral part of the article, a publisher wouldn't even try to take the link out... even though it takes people straight to my site where they can also join my affiliate program and see all of my products showcased.

Another way to use these "free stuff" links uses a web page with a free example on it, valuable free report, or whatever you give away for free and have a pop-under page that makes an offer for them to sign up to your list or buy your ebook.

Example from an actual article:

> Notice how the link takes you to a page where you can see the affiliate ID in your web browser's address bar. Like it or not, someone can replace my 'ebookfire' affiliate ID with their ID and "hijack" the commission... but at least the redirect script keeps them from seeing it in any email I send them.
>
> You can get free redirect scripts just about anywhere you find free java scripts. Here is the script I use:
>
> http://www.ebookfire.com/jrs.shtml

CAUTION: Do NOT abuse this technique #2 above… make sure the web page that pops under doesn't have all kinds of other pop-ups flying off. Launching people into "pop-up hell" doesn't get them to buy.

Sleeper Link #3 – "Curiosity" Link – you usually use this technique once you have built up someone's interest level to a fever pitch or you've gotten them to the point where they really want to know more about whatever you wrote about in your article. You can use verbiage such as "To see a really great example of this technique in action click here," or "To see what I'm talking about check this out => link."

This example comes from a free report I offer at http://www.ebookfire.com/fsbohelpcasestudy.shtml. By the way, this free report started out as an article and I simply expanded it into a free report.

> Oh, by the way, the man's name who taught me how to write this one-page sales letter that set me on the path that changed my life?
>
> Click this link to find out who he is and see the actual program he taught me that I used to create my one-page sales letter!

Click Here => <u>The Man Who Taught Me How to Write Sales Copy</u>

Final note...

It is my sincere hope that this "case study" will inspire you to create and build your own automated on-line business that generates real cash by selling ebooks.

Bottom Line with "Sleeper Links": The main idea behind sleeper links is that you want to have people click off your article from other places besides just the resource box. By doing so you will bypass many of their psychological defenses and make more sales and / or gather additional subscribers. Just don't make it really obvious and you should get good results.

Conclusion

Well, there you have it! You now possess a complete roadmap for conceiving, writing and promoting your business with articles on the Web. WOW!

Everything you just read came straight off the front lines of our experience on the Internet. We have proven and "battle tested" every technique and strategy.

Not one ounce of theory…

Not one ounce of fluff…

Just the facts and nothing but the facts about exactly what to do and how to do it when it comes to promoting with articles online!

Now, go do it!

You have the tools to make it happen and drive thousands of visitors to your website without paying a dime up front for them. Getting traffic with free articles rates just about the best website traffic you can get… so go get some!

Drop us a line and let us know how you do.

Thanks again – Happy Publishing!

To your success,

Jim & Dallas Edwards

Printed in the USA
CPSIA information can be obtained
at www.ICGtesting.com
JSHW082202140824
68134JS00014B/391

9 781600 371516